FROM 1910 TO THE PRESENT DAY

BRITISH CARS

FROM 1910 TO THE PRESENT DAY
BRITISH CARS

GENERAL EDITOR: CRAIG CHEETHAM

amber
BOOKS

First published in 2006 by
Amber Books Ltd
Bradley's Close
74–77 White Lion Street
London N1 9PF
United Kingdom
www.amberbooks.co.uk

ISBN-13: 978-1-905704-05-7
ISBN-10: 1-905704-05-4

Distributed in the UK by
Bookmart Ltd
Blaby Road
Wigston
Leicester LE18 4SE

Project Editor: Michael Spilling
Copy Editor: Caroline Curtis
Design: EQ Media

Printed in Dubai

CONTENTS

Introduction

IT MAY BE A SMALL COUNTRY, but that has not stopped the United Kingdom from making a significant contribution to the world's auto industry over more than a course of a century. Britain has a long and pioneering history of car manufacturing, from the very earliest days of motoring right through to the present. Over that time, the British Isles has created some of the world's most distinguished and respected marques, from the humble Austin and Morris brands right through to desirable, luxury names such as Aston Martin, Jaguar, Bentley and Rolls-Royce.

British Cars pays tribute to these vehicles, from early models such as the Le Mans-winning Bentley 4.5-Litre, through design classics such as the original Austin Mini and Morris Minor, right up to modern sports cars such as the TVR Chimaera and Lotus Elise. Inside this book you will find detailed descriptions and beautiful photography, bringing to life a broad

When TVR introduced the Cebera in 1996, it was a new departure for the British sports car maker. The curvy supercar included an inhouse 4.1l (251ci) engine, rather than the usual Rover V8. And just a year later, TVR added a 4.5l (273ci) engine, offering even more power.

cross-section of Britain's motoring icons. You will be able to appreciate the incredible use of space and intelligent design that marked out the very first Mini, the technological tour de force that was the Jaguar XJ220 and the sheer brute force of true 'British Bulldogs', such as the Lotus Omega, Jensen Interceptor and TVR Griffith.

Rise and Decline
But more than this, the book is a celebration of Britain's motor industry. This industry started in the garages and backyards of amateur mechanics and grew, at one time, to be the second largest in the world behind the United States. It is hard to believe it now, but Britain's car makers dominated the European market in the 1950s, while some models, such as the iconic MGB and Austin-Healey sports cars, even led their market classes in North America. After World War II, Britain's 'export-or-die' philosophy led to a massive growth in the motor industry and a worldwide respect for the country's tough, well-engineered and immaculately styled cars.

All good things come to an end, however, and following the dark recessions of the 1970s, when Britain's car factories were hit by labour unrest,

strikes and a sizeable downturn in quality, much of the homegrown industry failed to recover. Famous names such as Austin, Morris, Riley, Woleseley, Alvis and Triumph fell by the wayside, to be joined, much more recently, by Rover and MG. Today, these beautiful cars are distant memories, but their spirit lives on among Britain's army of classic car enthusiasts, dedicated to their remembrance and preservation.

Britain still produces a large number of cars, but as part of the globalization of the world's auto industry: today, the companies that build cars in Britain are global brands. Combined, General Motors, Nissan, Toyota and Honda still make over a million cars a year on British soil, but it is the smaller sports car makers like TVR, Caterham and Lotus that typify what the British motor industry really stands for.

Luxury Motoring

Much of the appeal of owning a British car, regardless of its age, lies in its classic style and attention to detail. While the collection of 42 cars celebrated in this book is by no means exhaustive, it catalogues some of the most significant cars not just in Britain's motoring history, but in that of the world.

British Cars looks in detail at some of the finest luxury models ever created. The stunning five-view photography puts you so close to the car that you can practically smell the leather, walnut veneer trim

First unveiled in 2000, the Aston Martin Vanquish showcased the classic car manufacturer's capabilities in the twenty-first century. Larger than its smaller brother, the DB7, the Vanquish had more cabin space, a lighter, carbon-fibre body and a powerful 6-litre (356ci) engine that could take the car up to 305km/h (190mph).

and deep-pile carpets that characterise a Jaguar XJ6, almost hear the purr that symbolizes a Bentley Continental R, or hear the late Eighties pop music blaring from the stereo of the MG Maestro Turbo.

The photography also allows you to inspect in detail the clever manufacturing techniques employed by the likes of TVR and Lotus to make their cars as light, strong and fast as possible. It is no coincidence that over 80 per cent of the world's motorsport engineers are British or British-based, and beautifully constructed cars such as these prove that the spirit of fine engineering – along with an unflinching enthusiasm for the automobile – is still alive and well in Britain.

Each of the cars in this book is described in loving detail, with genuine behind-the-wheel driving impressions from writers who have driven and compared the cars first hand. The thorough descriptions are backed up by comprehensive technical specifications, along with key dates in each car's history and a host of facts and trivia about each model to keep even the most ardent car enthusiast happy. We trust you will enjoy the ride.

AC **3000ME**

Based on the Diablo show car designed by Peter Bohanna, the 3000ME marked a return to true sports machines for Britain's oldest car maker. It suffered from development problems, however, and only a small number were built.

"*...superbly responsive.*"

"Compact is that word that best describes the 3000ME on first sight. Its cockpit is a fairly tight squeeze, but the interior is neatly laid out and well equipped. Acceleration is good, but not outstanding, with 0–96km/h (0–60mph) taking 9.0 seconds. Thanks to its mid-engined layout and all-independent suspension, it corners nicely. The rack-and-pinion steering is superbly responsive, and disc brakes at all corners enable rapid stops to be made."

For a mid-engined sports car, the 3000ME has a well-appointed and well-trimmed cabin.

Milestones

1972 Peter Bohanna
pens a stylish two-seater mid-engined roadster – the Diablo – which is intended to be powered by an Austin Maxi 1750-cc (107-ci) engine. On a trip to AC Cars, the Diablo catches Derek Hurlock's eye and the company decides to build a version of it using the Ford 3.0-litre V6 engine.

Fitting a Ford V8 engine into the Ace sports car resulted in the fearsome Cobra.

1979 After a
lengthy development period, the production car – the 3000ME – finally goes on sale.

AC's latest creation using Ford power is the Ace luxury GT.

1984 With only 70
cars having been built, AC Cars Scotland takes over 3000ME production. Although press reviews are favourable, sales are sluggish and production ends in 1985 after some 30 cars have left the Scottish factory.

UNDER THE SKIN

A mixed bag

Unlike previous ACs, the 3000ME has a pressed-steel perimeter frame chassis, onto which the fibreglass body is mounted. Positioning the engine centrally required a specially designed Hewland geared transmission to take drive to the rear wheels. For optimum handling, a double wishbone suspension is employed front and rear, although poor rear suspension geometry results in tricky handling at the limit.

Steel perimeter chassis

Four-wheel disc brakes

Double wishbone suspension

3.0-litre Ford V6

THE POWER PACK

Hydraulic lifters

Two valves per cylinder

Cast-iron block and cylinder heads

Five main-bearing crankshaft

Gutsy V6

It had originally been intended to use the 1750cc (107ci) in-line four from the Austin Maxi sedan, but once AC took over, the company decided to adopt the Ford 3.0-litre V6 Essex engine used in the Capri and Consul/Granada. A cast-iron unit with two valves per cylinder, it had a long-stroke design that resulted in a substantial amount of torque (174lb-ft at 3000rpm), but it was also easy to tweak for more horsepower. When fitted with a turbocharger, the power output jumped from 138bhp to a healthy 200bhp.

Turbocharged

Although the standard 3000ME was a decent performer in its day, Rooster Turbos later converted a small number of cars to turbocharged power. With 200bhp and improved suspension, they are more invigorating to drive than stock 3000MEs.

A small number of 3000MEs were reworked with turbocharged power.

AC **3000ME**

It seemed like the 3000ME, with its fibreglass body, racing-style suspension and reliable Ford V6 power, would be the answer to AC's problems. Alas, it took so long for the car to enter production that interest waned and only 70 were built.

Luggage space

With the engine mid-mounted, the luggage is carried up front. However, the small lid hinders access.

Fibreglass body

Unlike previous ACs, which had aluminium or steel bodies, the 3000ME has a fibreglass shell. This was cheap to manufacture and allowed considerable weight savings to be made.

Steel-perimeter chassis

A huge perimeter steel chassis was a first for AC. This makes the 3000ME very strong, but a side effect is too much weight and thus performance is adequate rather than sporty.

Hewland transmission

Because the V6 sat virtually on top of the transmission, AC had to design a new sump/transmission casing to house the Hewland gears. Unusually, drive is taken through a triple-row chain.

Protruding air cleaner

Because the V6 is shoehorned in, it protrudes from the rear bodywork. AC therefore fabricated a special external air cleaner to cover the carburetor.

Front radiator

The radiator is mounted at the front in the usual way, and the air forced through its large grille above the nose.

Stunning looks

The original Diablo created quite a stir, due mainly to its sleek shape. Not surprisingly, AC decided to leave the lines virtually unchanged for the production 3000ME.

Specifications

1979 AC 3000ME

ENGINE

Type: V6

Construction: Cast-iron block and heads

Valve gear: Two valves per cylinder operated by a single camshaft with pushrods and rockers

Bore and stroke: 94mm (3.7in) x 72mm (2.85in)

Displacement: 2994cc (182ci)

Compression ratio: 8.9:1

Induction system: Weber carburetor

Maximum power: 138bhp at 5000rpm

Maximum torque: 174lb-ft at 3000rpm

Top speed: 193km/h (120mph)

0–96km (0–60mph): 9.0 sec

TRANSMISSION

Five-speed manual

BODY/CHASSIS

Steel perimeter chassis with fibreglass two-door body

SPECIAL FEATURES

These vents are functional air extractor units.

RUNNING GEAR

Steering: Rack-and-pinion

Front suspension: Double wishbones with coil springs and telescopic shock absorbers

Rear suspension: Double wishbones with coil springs and telescopic shock absorbers

Brakes: Discs (front and rear)

Wheels: Forged magnesium, 17.8cm (7in) x 35.5cm (14in)

Tyres: 195/60HR16

DIMENSIONS

Length: 4m (157in)
Width: 1.65m (65in)

Height: 1.14m (45in)

Wheelbase: 228cm (90.5in)

Track: 136cm (55in) (front)
144cm (56.8in) (rear)

Weight: 1126kg (2483lbs)

11

Alvis **TD21**

In the early 1960s, if you couldn't afford a Bentley or a Rolls-Royce and thought Jaguars were too common and cheap, the perfect alternative was an Alvis. It had outstanding quality, a famous name and exclusivity.

"...excellent ride and handling."

"Alvis TD21 buyers wanted a driving experience rather than outright speed or acceleration, although both of these were perfectly adequate. The experience comes from a luxury interior, good looks and an excellent combination of ride and handling. Steering is sensitive and accurate and the whole car responds more like a 1960s' sports car than an elegant carriage. The ride is supple and relaxing, and the disc brakes are very effective."

Plenty of wood and leather gives the Alvis a really classy atmosphere inside.

Milestones

1955 Swiss coachbuilder

Graber shows a sport sedan based on the Alvis TC21 chassis. It inspires Alvis to build a similar model in England, but only 16 are made.

The TC21 was a much more traditional, upright car.

1958 The Graber styling

is used for the TD21. It is built as a two-door hardtop and a convertible.

The TD21 was replaced by the TE21 with stacked headlights.

1962 Substantial changes result

in the Mk II. It has Dunlop four-wheel disc brakes rather than front discs and rear drums, the rear lights are restyled and a ZF five-speed manual transmission is added.

1964 The TD21 is replaced

by the new and restyled TE21.

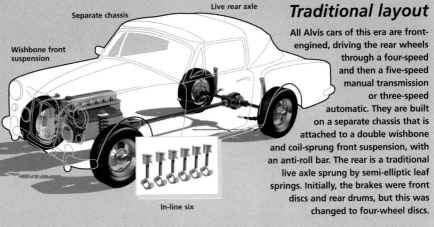

Separate chassis

Live rear axle

Wishbone front suspension

In-line six

Traditional layout

All Alvis cars of this era are front-engined, driving the rear wheels through a four-speed and then a five-speed manual transmission or three-speed automatic. They are built on a separate chassis that is attached to a double wishbone and coil-sprung front suspension, with an anti-roll bar. The rear is a traditional live axle sprung by semi-elliptic leaf springs. Initially, the brakes were front discs and rear drums, but this was changed to four-wheel discs.

THE POWER PACK

Simple six

Alvis' in-line six-cylinder engine dates back to 1950, when the Alvis TA21 was launched. It is a simple design with a cast-iron block and head. There are only two overhead valves per cylinder, operated by a single camshaft in the block via pushrods and rockers. It is not a cross-flow design, and so the inlet and exhaust manifolds are on the same side of the engine, compromising the engine's breathing and efficiency. It is, however, very strong and smooth and produces masses of torque.

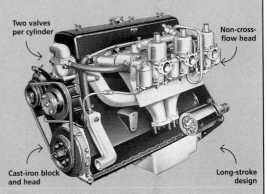

Two valves per cylinder

Non-cross-flow head

Cast-iron block and head

Long-stroke design

Swiss styling

Perhaps the most elegant of the TC to TF21 variants are the original Graber-bodied cars. The Swiss coachbuilder had been building sedans on the TC21 chassis for some time before Alvis took up the gauntlet. The first of the Alvis-commissioned cars had bodies built by the English firm Willowbrook, although Park Ward took over almost immediately.

Swiss-built Graber cars are the rarest and purest.

Alvis **TD21**

The elegant look of the TD21 was all thanks to the Swiss coachbuilder Hermann Graber, who had been building his own design on an Alvis chassis since the early 1950s.

Recirculating-ball steering
You might expect a car of the Alvis' class to have rack-and-pinion steering, but it used an unassisted recirculating-ball system. By 1965, the car could be ordered with ZF power steering.

In-line six-cylinder
Alvis steadily increased the power of its conventional in-line six-cylinder all-iron engine from just 90bhp in 1950. By the time the TD21 was made, the output had risen to 115bhp, thanks to a higher compression and twin carburetors.

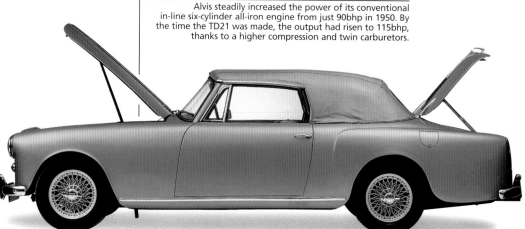

Separate chassis
There is nothing particularly complicated about the Alvis chassis; it is a conventional ladder-type frame with crossmembers. Because the car had a separate chassis, it was easier to make a convertible version.

Alloy bodywork
The Alvis bodies were coachbuilt and very labour-intensive. They are made from a mixture of aluminium and steel. The boot and bonnet are alloy, and the first TD21s had steel doors. For the Mk II, they were changed to alloy frames and skins.

Wooden frame
Until 1963, Alvis still used a lot of wooden framing in the old-fashioned way to make the bodies. The windshield pillars are made of solid ash, as are the door posts and the door frames.

Live axle
The conventional live rear axle is sprung by semi-elliptic leaf springs.

Specifications
1962 Alvis TD21

ENGINE

Type: In-line straight six-cylinder

Construction: Cast-iron block and head

Valve gear: Two valves per cylinder operated by a block-mounted camshaft with pushrods and rockers

Bore and stroke: 84mm (3.31in) x 90mm (3.54in)

Displacement: 2993cc (183ci)

Compression ratio: 8.5:1

Induction system: Twin SU carburetors

Maximum power: 115bhp at 4,000rpm

Maximum torque: 152lb-ft at 2,500rpm

Top Speed: 171km/h (106mph)

0–96km/h (0–60mph): 13.5 sec

TRANSMISSION

ZF five-speed manual

BODY/CHASSIS

Steel chassis with four-seater closed or open body

SPECIAL FEATURES

Late model TD21s were bodied by famous coachbuilders Park Ward.

The chrome wire wheels are knock-on for easy wheel changes.

RUNNING GEAR

Steering: Recirculating ball

Front suspension: Double wishbones with coil springs, telescopic shock absorbers and anti-roll bar

Rear suspension: Live axle with semi-elliptic leaf springs and telescopic shock absorbers

Brakes: Dunlop discs, 29.2cm (11.5in) dia. (front), 27.9cm (11.0-in) dia. (rear)

Wheels: Wire spoke, 4.5 x 15in

Tyres: Dunlop RS5 crossply, 600 x 38.1cm (15 in)

DIMENSIONS

Length: 4.8m (189.0in)

Width: 1.68m (66.0in)

Height: 1.5m (58.0in)

Wheelbase: 283cm (111.5in)

Track: 138cm (54.5in) (front and rear)

Weight: 1524kg (3360lbs)

Aston Martin **DB4 GT ZAGATO**

Aston Martin's DB4 GT was too heavy to be competitive, so it was given lightweight and aerodynamic Italian Zagato bodywork. With its 3.7-litre, six-cylinder engine tuned to 314bhp, a 241km/h (150mph) supercar was born.

"...fast and exciting road car."

"The DB4 GT Zagato is a racer that doubles as a fast and exciting road car. Given its high state of tune, the engine doesn't behave too badly. It has a lumpy idle, but when the revs are up it becomes obvious that this noisy powerplant means business. The gearshifter can be obstructive, though it becomes much easier with familiarity. The Zagato's performance is astounding, with a top speed of 245km/h (152mph) and hitting 160km/h (100mph) in less than 14 seconds."

The leather trimmed interior is attractive and all the gauges are easy to read.

Milestones

1958 Aston Martin

launches the DB4. Its 3.7-litre, 240-bhp engine gives astounding performance figures. It is sold alongside its predecessor, the DB Mark III.

Aston Martin's racer from the mid-1950s was the DB3S.

1959 The DB4 GT

debuts at the London Motor Show. Gianni Zagato meets John Wyer, Aston Martin's general manager.

1960 A chassis is sent to the Zagato factory on the outskirts of Milan, where it is given a new skin. Power is now up to 314bhp.

The standard DB4 is longer and heavier than the DB4 GT.

1961 Two factory cars enter the Le Mans 24 Hours race. Unfortunately, both of them retire early.

1963 Production ends and Aston Martin now has a more specialized racer.

UNDER THE SKIN

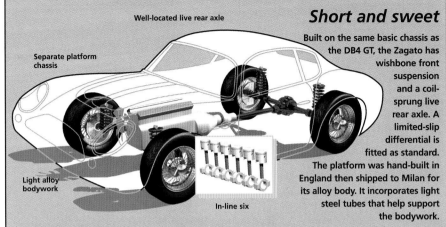

Well-located live rear axle

Separate platform chassis

Light alloy bodywork

In-line six

Short and sweet

Built on the same basic chassis as the DB4 GT, the Zagato has wishbone front suspension and a coil-sprung live rear axle. A limited-slip differential is fitted as standard. The platform was hand-built in England then shipped to Milan for its alloy body. It incorporates light steel tubes that help support the bodywork.

THE POWER PACK

Highly tuned

The starting point for the Zagato engine was the DB4 GT unit, which was in turn derived from the DB4's new in-line twin-cam six. It has a capacity of 3670cc (224ci) from the square bore and stroke dimensions of 92mm (3.62in) x 92mm (3.62in). The all-alloy engine has chain-driven camshafts operating two valves per cylinder in the cross-flow head with hemispherical combustion chambers. The GT unit has an increased compression ratio, higher-lift cams, three carburetors and two spark plugs per cylinder.

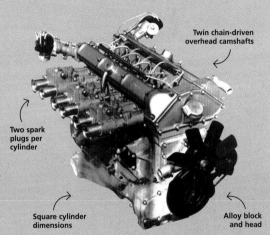

Twin chain-driven overhead camshafts

Two spark plugs per cylinder

Square cylinder dimensions

Alloy block and head

Racer returns

When the original run of 19 Zagatos had been completed, four chassis numbers allocated to the model were left over. In 1991, these remaining chassis numbers were used on near-exact replicas, known as Sanction II cars, which were approved by Aston Martin and built with the help of Zagato.

The Sanction II DB4 GT Zagatos are more powerful than the original cars.

Aston Martin **DB4 GT ZAGATO**

When Aston Martin wanted to beat Ferrari's 250 GT SWB, the company needed something even more special than its 302-bhp DB4 GT. The result was the sensational-looking DB4 GT Zagato.

Independent front suspension

The DB4 GT has a double wishbone assembly with a particularly wide lower link. An anti-roll bar improves the car's cornering.

Thoroughbred six-cylinder engine

The highly-tuned, all-alloy, 3670cc (224ci) straight-six engine has twin overhead camshafts and two spark plugs per cylinder.

Alloy-rim wire wheels

Centre-lock Borrani wire wheels are fitted as standard, with alloy rims to reduce weight. The wheels have 72 spokes—a larger number than usual—to cope with the engine's 278lb-ft of torque.

Lightweight Perspex windows

To keep weight to a minimum, the Zagato has Perspex side and rear windows.

Specifications

1962 Aston Martin DB4 GT Zagato

ENGINE

Type: In-line six-cylinder

Construction: Alloy block and head

Valve gear: Two valves per cylinder operated by twin overhead camshafts

Bore and stroke: 92mm (3.62in) x 92mm (3.62in)

Displacement: 3670cc (224ci)

Compression ratio: 9.7:1

Induction system: Three twin-choke sidedraft carburetors

Maximum power: 314bhp at 6000rpm

Maximum torque: 278lb-ft at 5400rpm

Top Speed: 245km/h (152mph)

0–96km/h (0–60mph): 6.1 sec

TRANSMISSION

Four-speed manual

BODY/CHASSIS

Separate box-section chassis with alloy two-door coupé body

SPECIAL FEATURES

Twin exhausts help to expel combustion gases as efficiently as possible.

RUNNING GEAR

Steering: Rack-and-pinion

Front suspension: Double wishbones with coil springs and telescopic shocks

Rear suspension: Live axle with radius arms, Watt's link, coil springs and telescopic shocks

Brakes: Discs, 30.5cm (12in) dia. (front), 28cm (11in) dia. (rear)

Wheels: Borrani centre-lock wire wheels

Tyres: Avon Turbospeed Mk II, 15.2cm (6in) x 40.6cm (16in)

DIMENSIONS

Length: 4.3m (168in)

Width: 1.65m (65.3in)

Height: 1.27m (50in)

Wheelbase: 236cm (93in)

Track: 138cm (54.4in) (front), 138.4cm (54.5in) (rear)

Weight: 1254kg (2765lbs)

Short wheelbase

The DB4 GT Zagato (and DB4 GT) has a wheelbase that is 12.7cm (5in) shorter than the standard four-seater DB4, thus reducing weight.

Aston Martin **DB6**

Few cars are so quintessentially British as the Aston Martin DB6. Elegance, hand-built craftsmanship, power, ruggedness and charm combine to produce a wonderful expression of classic Gran Turismo qualities.

"...a magical drive."

"Step inside the DB6, and the smell of the leather upholstery, the feel of the wood-rimmed steering wheel and the cluster of gauges tell you that this is going to be a magical drive. There is a lot of power under your right foot, and despite its bulk, the DB6 is surprisingly quick off the line. The handling is old-fashioned but faithful. It is fast through the gears and stops quickly and very straight."

The DB6 has one of the greatest interiors of all British classic cars. Dashboard, carpets and trim all exude quality.

Milestones

1965 The new DB6 is launched to replace the DB5. Unlike the DB5, it uses a more modern monocoque construction. Its cut-off tail improves aerodynamics, increasing top speed despite the extra weight.

The open-top Volante is the most valuable DB6 model.

1969 A DB6 Mk 2 is introduced. It has DBS-style wider wheels and flared arches, as well as power steering and the option of fuel injection.

Aston Martin revived the famous DB line with the DB7, which was launched in 1994.

1970 Production draws to a close and the DB6 retires as the most popular Aston Martin yet made. Its replacement, the DBS, has been in production since 1967. The DBS V8 is the last of the DB line until the arrival of the DB7 in 1994.

UNDER THE SKIN

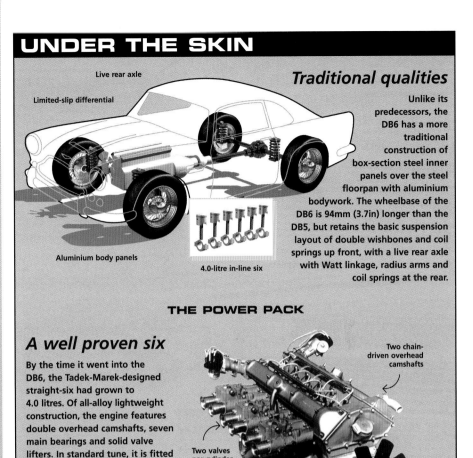

Live rear axle

Limited-slip differential

Aluminium body panels

4.0-litre in-line six

Traditional qualities

Unlike its predecessors, the DB6 has a more traditional construction of box-section steel inner panels over the steel floorpan with aluminium bodywork. The wheelbase of the DB6 is 94mm (3.7in) longer than the DB5, but retains the basic suspension layout of double wishbones and coil springs up front, with a live rear axle with Watt linkage, radius arms and coil springs at the rear.

THE POWER PACK

A well proven six

By the time it went into the DB6, the Tadek-Marek-designed straight-six had grown to 4.0 litres. Of all-alloy lightweight construction, the engine features double overhead camshafts, seven main bearings and solid valve lifters. In standard tune, it is fitted with three SU carburetors and develops 282bhp. The very popular Vantage engine option has triple twin-choke Weber 45DCOE carburetors and pumps out 325bhp at 5750rpm.

Two chain-driven overhead camshafts

Two valves per cylinder

Seven main bearings

All-alloy construction

Best choice

The Vantage engine, with its extra power and performance, is the obvious power unit to choose. Although the coupé is graceful, the Volante convertible is a timeless design. Its electric roof folds neatly away at the touch of a button.

The cut-off tail with lip spoiler is a DB6 trademark.

Aston Martin **DB6**

With its graceful lines, elegant interior and sophisticated mechanics, the DB6 lived up to the Aston Martin reputation of providing expensive upper-class Grand Touring cars.

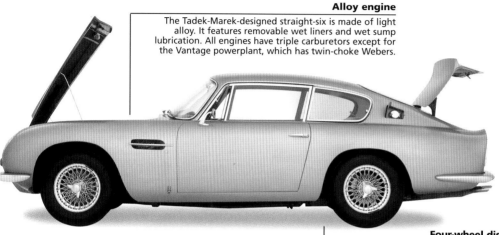

Alloy engine

The Tadek-Marek-designed straight-six is made of light alloy. It features removable wet liners and wet sump lubrication. All engines have triple carburetors except for the Vantage powerplant, which has twin-choke Webers.

Four-wheel disc brakes

To stop more than 1360kg (3000lbs) from speeds approaching 241km/h (150mph), disc brakes are necessary. They are substantial and are clearly visible through the chromed wire wheels.

Kamm tail

While the DB6's rear end styling may lack the purity of line of the original DB4/DB5 design by Touring of Milan, it certainly helps aerodynamics. The raised rear lip forms a spoiler and halves the aerodynamic lift on the rear end, thereby boosting high-speed stability.

Choice of body styles

The most popular body style is the fastback sedan, of which 1567 were made between 1965 and 1970. The desirable Volante convertible is much rarer – only 215 were built.

Luxurious interior

The interior is of the highest quality. Wall-to-wall carpeting, rich leather upholstery, multiple gauges and a racing-style wood/metal sandwich steering wheel are just some of its features.

Specifications

1965 Aston Martin DB6 Vantage

ENGINE

Type: In-line six-cylinder

Construction: Aluminium block and head

Valve gear: Two valves per cylinder operated by double overhead camshafts

Bore and stroke: 96mm (3.77in) x 92mm (3.62in)

Displacement: 3995cc (244ci)

Compression ratio: 8.9:1

Induction system: Three twin-choke Weber carburetors

Maximum power: 325bhp at 5750rpm

Maximum torque: 290lb-ft at 4500rpm

Top speed: 241km/h (150mph)

0–96km (0–60mph): 6.7 sec

TRANSMISSION

Five-speed manual or three-speed automatic

BODY/CHASSIS

Integral steel chassis with two-door aluminium coupé or convertible body

SPECIAL FEATURES

The wire wheels are held on by central spinners, which have to be knocked off using a special mallet.

RUNNING GEAR

Steering: Rack-and-pinion

Front suspension: Double wishbones with coil springs, telescopic shocks and anti-roll bar

Rear suspension: Live axle with radius arms, Watt linkage, telescopic shocks and coil springs

Brakes: Discs (front and rear)

Wheels: Spoked, 38.1cm (15in) dia.

Tyres: 6.70 x 15in

DIMENSIONS

Length: 4.62m (182in)

Width: 1.68m (66in)

Height: 1.32m (52in)

Wheelbase: 259cm (101.8in)

Track: 137cm (54in) (front), 136cm (53.5in) (rear)

Weight: 1550kg (3418lbs)

ASTON MARTIN **DB7**

With Ford's money behind the company, Aston Martin was at last able to build a worthy successor to the DB5 and DB6 of the 1960s, fast and beautiful in the true Aston tradition.

"Supercharged sophistication."

"You soon see why the Aston is so expensive; the chassis is simply wonderful, enabling the DB7 to tackle tight corners, sweeping curves, off camber bends – it's all the same to the Aston and it does it with the same finesse as a Jaguar. It's got enough power to push the back end out, but it does it in a very controlled way. And thanks to powerful brakes and the instant power that the super-charger makes available, the Aston's combination is perfect."

The modern and stylish interior is comfortable as well as functional.

Milestones

1965 Last of the numbered
DB series, the DB6, appears, named after Aston Martin owner David Brown. The DB6's successor, the DBS, uses a V8 engine, ending the six-cylinder line until the current car appears.

The sporty DB7 is the spiritual successor to the famous DB6 of the 1960s.

1992 Aston Martin Oxford Ltd.
is formed to produce a new Aston Martin. Mechanically, it is closely related to the Jaguar XJS because now Aston Martin and Jaguar are both part of Ford.

The DB7 was originally for Jaguar, and at the last hour was used for Aston Martin.

1994 The DB7
makes its debut.

1996 Two more years of development
results in the DB7 Volante model with its power convertible top, intended primarily for the US market.

UNDER THE SKIN

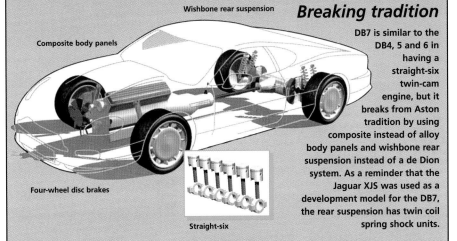

Wishbone rear suspension

Composite body panels

Four-wheel disc brakes

Straight-six

Breaking tradition

DB7 is similar to the DB4, 5 and 6 in having a straight-six twin-cam engine, but it breaks from Aston tradition by using composite instead of alloy body panels and wishbone rear suspension instead of a de Dion system. As a reminder that the Jaguar XJS was used as a development model for the DB7, the rear suspension has twin coil spring shock units.

THE POWER PACK

Supercharged six

Thanks to its mechanically driven Eaton supercharger, the 3.2-litre all-alloy straight-six, twin-cam 24-valve engine, developed with the help of TWR, produces more than 100bhp per litre, the sign of a true high-performance engine. The supercharger also helps to give a vast amount of low-down torque as well as outright power, and the maximum torque is produced at only 3000rpm.

Twin camshafts

Alloy block and heads

Eaton supercharger

Chop top

Two years after the DB7 first appeared, Aston Martin introduced the Volante convertible model. It's a bit heavier and slower and has softer, more compliant suspension, but the attraction of top-down supercar motoring overcomes the drawbacks.

Volante is the traditional name Aston Martin gives to its convertible models.

ASTON MARTIN **DB7**

With the DB7, Aston Martin discarded the brutal appearance of its V8 range in favour of a smooth, sleek look designed in Britain. Its beauty did not hide the fact it was a seriously fast car, though.

Fibreglass bodywork

The DB7 would be even heavier if it had conventional steel body panels. The fibreglass bodywork is lighter than steel and also cheaper to produce than the hand-finished alloy panels of traditional Aston Martins.

Straight-six engine

The DB7's short-stroke engine is an in-line six-cylinder with four valves per cylinder. At 3239cc (198ci), it's smaller but more powerful than any of the straight-six twin cams used in the previous DB range.

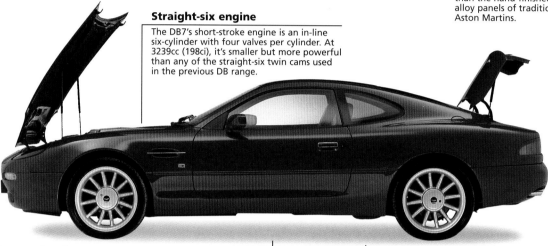

Same wheelbase as DB6

Curiously enough, the DB7 has exactly the same wheelbase as the old DB6, although the body is wider and longer and has a significantly wider track.

Outstanding brakes

Although only the front discs are vented, the DB7's brakes are absolutely outstanding and can stop the car from 96km/h (60mph) in only 2.8 seconds.

Leather interior

An Aston Martin wouldn't be an Aston Martin without a luxurious interior and the DB7 features Connolly hide. It is available in bright two-tone finishes where the DBs of the 1960s were more restrained and less stylish.

Front-heavy weight distribution

Although the engine is all alloy, engine accessories like the supercharger and intercooler help tip the DB7's weight toward the front, giving a 54/46 front-to-rear distribution.

2+2 accommodation

Two rear passengers can just about be crammed into the upright rear seats with their very narrow seat bottoms, making the DB7 a 2+2.

Intercooler

Forced induction heats the intake air and thins it, so an intercooler is fitted to the supercharger, just as it is with a turbocharger, to cool the air before it reaches the engine, restoring its density and increasing the power the engine can produce.

Specifications
1997 Aston Martin DB7

ENGINE
Type: In-line six-cylinder
Construction: Alloy block and head
Valve gear: Four valves per cylinder operated by twin overhead camshafts
Bore and stroke: 91mm (3.58in) x 83mm (3.26in)
Displacement: 3239cc (198ci)
Compression ratio: 8.3:1
Induction system: Electronic sequential fuel injection with Eaton mechanical supercharger and intercooler
Maximum power: 335bhp at 5750rpm
Maximum torque: 400lb-ft at 3000rpm
Top speed: 406km/h (252mph)
0–96km (0–60mph): 6.0 sec

TRANSMISSION
Five-speed manual

BODY/CHASSIS
Steel floorpan with fibreglass 2+2 coupé body

SPECIAL FEATURES

Vents behind the front wheel arches are similar to the 1960s DB4, 5 and 6s.

A true 2+2, the DB7 has separate, small bucket seats for rear passengers.

RUNNING GEAR
Steering: Rack-and-pinion
Front suspension: Double wishbones, coil springs, telescopic shocks and anti-roll bar
Rear suspension: Double wishbones, coil springs, telescopic shocks and anti-roll bar
Brakes: Four-wheel discs, vented, 33.5cm (13.2in) dia. (front), solid 30.5cm (12in) dia. (rear); ABS
Wheels: Alloy, 20.3cm (8in) x 45.7cm (18in)
Tyres: 245/40 ZR18

DIMENSIONS
Length: 4.63m (182.3in)
Width: 1.82m (71.6in)
Height: 1.26m (49.8in)
Wheelbase: 259cm (102in)
Track: 152cm (60in) (front), 152cm (59.8in) (rear)
Weight: 1750kg (3858lbs)

Austin **MINI Mk 1**

Some people claim that the Mini is the most significant European car ever built. It was genuinely revolutionary: a tiny, front-wheel drive sedan that boasts zippy performance, sports car handling and unbeatable economy.

"...acceleration is surprising."

"There is no car like the Mini. You have to sort of hunch over to get into it. Its driving position with the large, upright steering wheel resembles that of a miniature bus. The engine turns over by pushing a button on the floor. Initial acceleration is surprising, and you will be amazed by its handling when you go through your first corner. Enzo Ferrari himself was impressed the first time he took the little car for a test drive."

A minimalist interior has helped earn the Mini cult status.

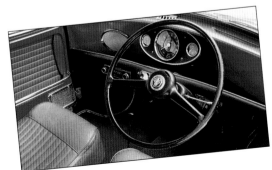

Milestones

1959 BMC launches a revolutionary new car under two nameplates: the Austin Seven and the Morris Mini Minor.

1961 A luxury Super model is launched with extra trim and a different grille. More important, the legendary Mini Cooper sports version is born.

John Lennon and Peter Sellers both owned Minis.

1962 The Seven name is dropped for Austin variants. It's now called just 'Mini.'

1964 The suspension is changed to a more pliant Hydrolastic fluid system.

The sporty Mini Cooper was an all-conquering giant beater.

1965 An automatic transmission option is available.

1967 Mk1s give way to the modified Mk2.

UNDER THE SKIN

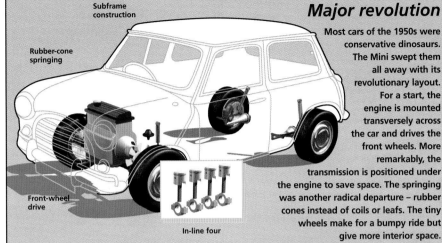

Subframe construction

Rubber-cone springing

Front-wheel drive

In-line four

Major revolution

Most cars of the 1950s were conservative dinosaurs. The Mini swept them all away with its revolutionary layout. For a start, the engine is mounted transversely across the car and drives the front wheels. More remarkably, the transmission is positioned under the engine to save space. The springing was another radical departure – rubber cones instead of coils or leafs. The tiny wheels make for a bumpy ride but give more interior space.

THE POWER PACK

Reliable A-series power

The Mini's engine is a direct development of the 803cc (49ci) A-series engine first used in the Austin A30. BMC engineers experimented with a bored-out 948cc (58ci) version, but they finally arrived at 848cc (52ci) by reducing the stroke. It is fed by a single SU carburetor. The humble 37bhp may not sound like much, but in a car weighing only 608kg (1340lbs) it is more than enough for adequate travel. The original A-series engine grew to 998cc (61ci) and then to 1275cc (78ci) for the Mini Cooper S. Amazingly, the 1275cc (78ci) unit is still in production, now with fuel injection.

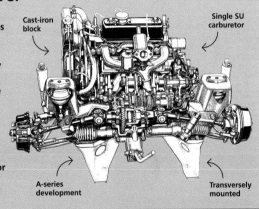

Cast-iron block

Single SU carburetor

A-series development

Transversely mounted

Mk1 marvel

There is something about the purity of the original Mini that is enchanting. If you are lucky enough to find an example from the first month of production, you will be sitting on a gold mine—some have been known to sell for more than $10,000.

Very early examples of the Mk1 in good condition are quite valuable.

Austin **MINI Mk 1** 🇬🇧

The Mini changed the face of driving in Europe and became a popular low budget car. Simple and cleverly engineered, it turned into one of the best-selling British cars ever made.

Transmission mounted under engine

One of the most revolutionary aspects of the Mini was the fact that the transmission is mounted under the engine's crankshaft, giving a very compact powertrain.

Subframe construction

To deal with vibration and to make the packaging more versatile, all of the major components – engine, steering, transmission and front suspension – are mounted together on the front subframe.

Tiny wheels

The 25.4cm (10in) wheels on the Mini are the smallest of any car of its day (excluding bubble cars). The reason for such small wheels is that they intrude less on passenger space.

Boxy cabin

When he set about designing the Mini, engineer Alec Issigonis was obsessed by the need to save space. He established that the minimum area required for four passengers was a cube 2.64m (104in) long by 1.27m (50in) wide and 1.32m (52in) tall. This dictated the simple, boxy shape of the Mini, which is surprisingly roomy inside.

Useful boot

The boot may not be very large, but it can hold a lot thanks to the bottom-hinged tailgate.

Simple shape

The extremely simple profile of the Mini evolved entirely from engineering precepts. The man behind the Mini, Alec Issigonis, was anti-styling and resisted all attempts to make his car stylish. This is probably fortunate, as the Mini's shape is a timeless classic as a result.

Specifications

1959 Austin Seven

ENGINE

Type: In-line four-cylinder

Construction: Cast-iron block and head

Valve gear: Two valves per cylinder operated by a single camshaft

Bore and stroke: 63mm (2.48in) x 68mm (2.68in)

Displacement: 848cc (52ci)

Compression ratio: 8.3:1

Induction system: Single SU carburetor

Maximum power: 37bhp at 5500rpm

Maximum torque: 44lb-ft at 2900rpm

Top Speed: 121km/h (75mph)

0–96km/h (0–60mph): 26.5 sec

TRANSMISSION

Four-speed manual

BODY/CHASSIS

Unitary monocoque construction with subframes and steel two-door sedan body

SPECIAL FEATURES

The rounded design of the Mk1's grille is its most distinctive feature.

RUNNING GEAR

Steering: Rack-and-pinion

Front suspension: Wishbones with rubber cone springs and telescopic shock absorbers

Rear suspension: Trailing arms with rubber cone springs and telescopic shock absorbers

Brakes: Drums (front and rear)

Wheels: Steel, 25.4cm (10in) dia.

Tyres: 5.20 x 10

DIMENSIONS

Length: 3m (120.3in)

Width: 1.39m (55.0in)

Height: 1.34m (53.0in)

Wheelbase: 204cm (80.2in)

Track: 122cm (48.2in) (front), 117.3cm (46.2in) (rear)

Weight: 608kg (1340lbs)

Austin **MINI COOPER**

When Formula 1 constructor John Cooper showed that the basic Mini could be transformed with a more powerful engine and disc brakes, the startling result instantly became one of the world's best rally cars.

"...amazing handling."

"Forget the upright driving position with its horrible seats and buslike angle of the steering wheel. Dynamically, everything else about the Cooper S is perfect. It has immediate response to the steering, amazing handling characteristics, grip that was unmatched (even on those tiny tyres) and a feel that made you drive it absolutely flat out around every corner it met. The transmission howls and it's undergeared, which makes it too noisy for motorways, but it's in its element on twisty country roads and rally circuits."

It may not be too comfortable at the wheel of a Mini Cooper, but it's certainly entertaining.

Milestones

1959 Mini introduced
in Austin and Morris forms.

Issigonis' Mini soon showed a capability to take more power.

1961 First Mini Cooper appears with a
bigger engine and disc brakes.

1963 Cooper given 998-cc engine. First Mini
Cooper S is launched, with 1,031-cc (61-ci), 70-bhp engine. It is produced for just a year.

Mini Coopers had a huge impact on world rallying.

1964 Coopers given
998-cc engines and the new Hydrolastic suspension. The 970-cc Cooper S is built for homologation: only 963 are made. In March the 1,275-cc Cooper S appears with 76-bhp engine.

1970 MkII Cooper S
(essentially just a minor restyle launched in 1967) turns into the MkIII with better seats and wind-up windows.

UNDER THE SKIN

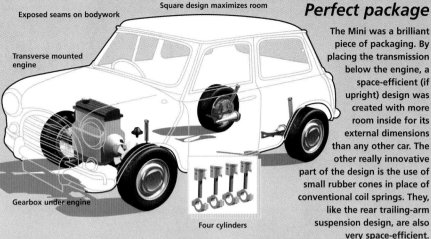

Exposed seams on bodywork

Square design maximizes room

Transverse mounted engine

Gearbox under engine

Four cylinders

Perfect package

The Mini was a brilliant piece of packaging. By placing the transmission below the engine, a space-efficient (if upright) design was created with more room inside for its external dimensions than any other car. The other really innovative part of the design is the use of small rubber cones in place of conventional coil springs. They, like the rear trailing-arm suspension design, are also very space-efficient.

THE POWER PACK

Tunable four

The A-series engine was an old design even when the Mini was new. It is a simple all-iron, overhead-valve design with in-line valves, and the carburetor and exhaust ports are on the same side of the head. The first Minis were 848cc (52ci) with 34bhp but the first Coopers had 997cc (60.8ci) and then 998cc (60.9ci) versions with twin carburetors and 55bhp. Biggest of the A-series variants was the 1275cc (78ci), which, in the Cooper S, produced 76bhp.

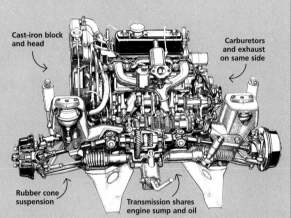

Cast-iron block and head

Carburetors and exhaust on same side

Rubber cone suspension

Transmission shares engine sump and oil

Superior S

The smaller-engined Coopers were fun, but the extra power and torque of the 1275cc (78ci) engine in the Cooper S and its better brakes makes it more desirable. For those who don't mind bouncing around, the original rubber cone suspended car is the one to have.

Cooper S was a match for far larger race and rally cars.

Austin **MINI COOPER S**

The Mini Cooper's amazing road holding comes from its wheel at each corner design and its light weight. It quickly became the best small sporting sedan in the world, at home on the race track as well as rally stage.

Sliding windows

Because the Mini was so narrow, and designed to be cheap, the windows were the cheaper sliding type so that the doors could be single skin and fitted with storage-useful pockets.

Transmission in sump

Placing the transmission below the engine meant that it had to share the engine's oil instead of the special high-pressure oil normally used for transmissions, but this was never a problem.

Disc brakes

All Coopers and Cooper Ss are fitted with front Lockhead disc brakes, the Cooper Ss with larger discs (18.9cm /7.48in diameter) than the 17.8cm (7in) discs fitted to the lesser-powered cars.

Small wheels

No other cars had been built with such tiny 25.4cm (10in) diameter wheels as the Mini. The tyres had to be made specially by Dunlop. In later years, after the Cooper went out of production, the Mini was equipped with taller wheels.

Hydrolastic suspension

In 1964, the rubber cone 'dry' suspension was replaced by the Hydrolastic type, in which a pressurized fluid-filled hydraulic unit supplies the springing for each wheel. Each front unit is interconnected to the corresponding rear unit so that no separate shocks are needed.

Side radiator

To keep the car as short as possible, there was no room for the radiator ahead of the engine and it is mounted to one side at right angles to the air stream, but it still functions adequately.

Rubber suspension

Early Coopers use special rubber cones instead of coil springs; compressing them had just the same effect, but they take up much less space.

Exposed side seams

The seams where the body panels join together were deliberately exposed on the outside and made into a styling feature.

Twin fuel tanks

The popular misconception is that all Cooper S models had twin fuel tanks, but in fact the right-hand tank was an option.

A-series engine

BMC's A-series engine may have been all cast iron, with a single block-mounted camshaft and two overhead valves per cylinder, but it was an excellent design with considerable tuning potential.

Specifications
1964 970-cc Mini Cooper S

ENGINE

Type: In-line four cylinder
Construction: Cast-iron block and head
Valve gear: Two in-line valves per cylinder operated by single block-mounted camshaft, pushrods and rockers
Bore and stroke: 71mm (2.78in) x 62mm (2.44in)
Displacement: 970cc (59ci)
Compression ratio: 9.75:1
Induction system: Two SU HS2 carburetors
Maximum power: 65bhp at 6500rpm
Maximum torque: 76lb-ft at 3500rpm
Top Speed: 156km/h (97mph)
0–96km (0–60mph): 10.9 sec

TRANSMISSION
Four-speed manual

BODY/CHASSIS
Steel monocoque two-door, four-seat sedan

SPECIAL FEATURES

The deliberately exposed seams on the bodywork became a Mini hallmark. External door hinges identify an early Mini.

To increase the Mini's carrying capacity, it could be driven with the boot lid half open.

RUNNING GEAR

Steering: Rack-and-pinion
Front suspension: Double wishbones with rubber cone springs and Girling telescopic shocks
Rear suspension: Longitudinal trailing arms, rubber cone springs and Girling telescopic shocks
Brakes: Discs (front), 18.9cm (7.48in), drums (rear)
Wheels: Steel, 11.4cm (4.5in) x 25.4cm (10in)
Tyres: Dunlop C41 5.20 x 10 or Dunlop SP41 145/10

DIMENSIONS

Length: 3m (120in)
Width: 1.4m (55.5in)
Height: 1.34m (3in)
Wheelbase: 203cm (80.1in)
Track: 121cm (47.5in) (front), 118cm (46.3in) (rear)
Weight: 578kg (1275lbs)

Austin-Healey **3000**

The combination of Austin's 3-litre engine and Donald Healey's sports car produced a rugged classic with enormous character and an impressive competition record.

"...it needs a firm hand."

"Healeys are not the easiest of cars to drive, as the 'works' rally drivers would testify. Steering is heavy and shifting is awkward (although flicking a switch in and out of overdrive is delightfully easy). The Healey's basic tendency is to go straight at corners, so it needs a firm hand. Bumpy roads will throw the stiffly sprung back axle off line, make the scuttle shake and the steering wheel kick. Apply too much power in corners and you easily trade understeer for oversteer, though that's just an accepted part of the car's character."

MkIII Austin-Healey 3000 has improved interior with a wooden dashboard.

Milestones

1952 Healey 100 is completed in time for the British Motor Show. It has a four-cylinder, 90-bhp Austin A90 engine. The design is built by BMC as an Austin-Healey.

1956 100 turns into the 100/6 when equipped with Austin's 2.6-litre, six-cylinder engine.

The 3000 was a great rally car. The fiercest of all 'works' cars were Mark IIIs with 210bhp.

1959 3000 introduced with power up to 124bhp.

1960 Proving what a great rally car the 3000 is, Pat Moss wins the Liege-Rome-Liege Rally.

1961 Power increases to 132bhp producing the 3000 MkII. A restyle takes place in the following year.

Austin-Healey experimented with a closed version of the 3000, but it never reached production.

1964 Definitive 3000, the MkIII appears. Rauno Aaltonen/Tony Ambrose win the Spa-Sofia-Liege rally in one.

UNDER THE SKIN

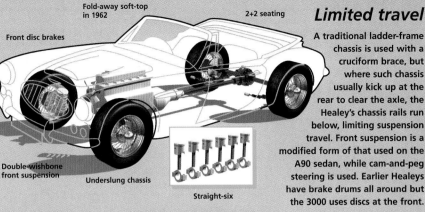

Fold-away soft-top in 1962

Front disc brakes

2+2 seating

Double-wishbone front suspension

Underslung chassis

Straight-six

THE POWER PACK

Limited travel

A traditional ladder-frame chassis is used with a cruciform brace, but where such chassis usually kick up at the rear to clear the axle, the Healey's chassis rails run below, limiting suspension travel. Front suspension is a modified form of that used on the A90 sedan, while cam-and-peg steering is used. Earlier Healeys have brake drums all around but the 3000 uses discs at the front.

C-Series improved

Healey modified the Austin C-Series engine built for sedans like the Austin A90. It has a cast-iron block and cylinder head with a single block-mounted camshaft and conventional rocker-driven overhead valves. The camshaft profile is modified and the cylinder head is improved to increase power, which ranges from the 124bhp of the Austin-Healey 100/6 to the 148bhp of the final 3000 variant, which could also boast 165lb-ft of torque. With triple Weber carburetors for competition, 210bhp is possible.

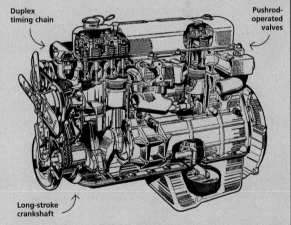

Duplex timing chain

Pushrod-operated valves

Long-stroke crankshaft

Ultimate mark

The last, the best, and definitely the fastest of the 3000 line is the MkIII. It has an improved interior, wooden dashboard, power up from 131bhp to 148bhp, plus a revised chassis that improves the rear suspension and better locates the back axle.

The best interior and most power make the MkIII the one to have.

Austin-Healey **3000**

This hybrid designed by Donald Healey and incorporating Austin running gear helped make the 3000 one of the greatest British sports cars ever assembled.

Knock-on wire wheels

Traditional knock-on centre-lock wire wheels are the usual fitment on the Austin-Healey, although bolt-on steel disc wheels were available.

Austin engine

All the 'Big Healeys', as they were commonly known, use modified cast-iron Austin engines. They are uncomplicated overhead-valve designs, but are tuneable and very strong.

Front disc brakes

Early Austin-Healeys were drum braked, but from 1959 more effective servo-assisted discs were fitted at the front.

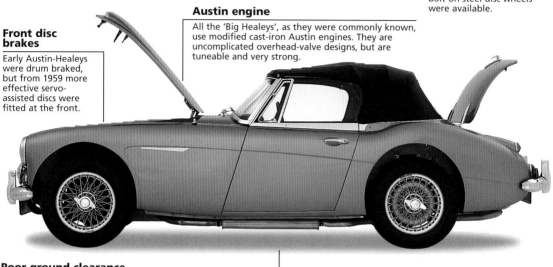

Poor ground clearance

Austin-Healeys are notorious for their poor ground clearance, and the exhaust system is particularly vulnerable. This was a great problem for the rally cars and one reason why clearance was improved in 1964.

Two-seaters and 2+2s

From 1962, the two-seater option was deleted and all the 3000 MkII and MkIII models were 2+2s, so occasional passengers could be squeezed in.

Live rear axle

Donald Healey did not want the expense and complication of independent rear suspension and used a live axle. At one time there was a Panhard rod, but that was discarded after 1964 and radius arms were fitted.

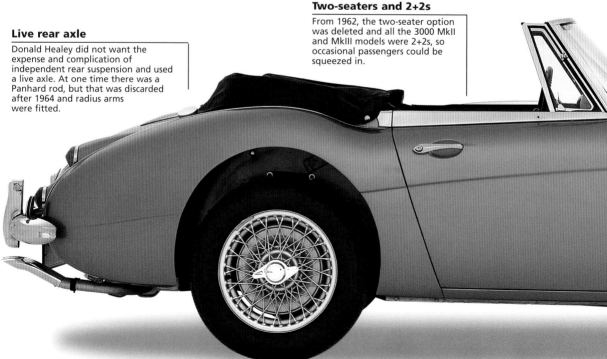

In-house styling

Donald Healey relied on his own company to style the original Healey 100, and much of that style lived on in the 3000.

Cam-and-peg steering

Although the smaller Austin-Healey Sprite uses rack-and-pinion steering, the 3000 has a less precise cam-and-peg system because it was easier to accommodate with the big six-cylinder engine.

Underslung chassis

The chassis was designed for a low, sleek look with the rear axle mounted above the chassis rails.

Specifications

1964 Austin-Healey 3000 MkIII

ENGINE

Type: In-line six cylinder
Construction: Cast-iron block and head
Valve gear: Two in-line valves per cylinder operated by single block-mounted camshaft, pushrods and rockers
Bore and stroke: 83mm (8.26in) x 89mm (3.50in)
Displacement: 2912cc (178ci)
Compression ratio: 9.0:1
Induction system: Two SU carburetors
Maximum power: 148bhp at 5250rpm
Maximum torque: 165lb-ft at 3500rpm
Top speed: 193km/h (120mph)
0–96km (0–60mph): not quoted

TRANSMISSION

Four-speed manual with overdrive on third and fourth gear

BODY/CHASSIS

X-braced ladder-frame chassis with steel 2+2 convertible body

SPECIAL FEATURES

The left-exiting exhaust shows that this is a left-hand-drive model. About 90 per cent of 3000s were exported.

RUNNING GEAR

Steering: Cam-and-peg
Front suspension: Double wishbones, coil springs, lever arm shocks and anti-roll bar
Rear suspension: Live axle with semi-elliptic leaf springs, lever arm shocks and radius arms
Brakes: Discs (front), drums (rear)
Wheels: Knock-on centre-lock wire spoke 11.4cm (4.5in) x 38.1cm (15in)
Tyres: Crossply 15cm (5.9in) x 38.1cm (15in)

DIMENSIONS

Length: 4m (157.5in)
Width: 1.54m (60.5in)
Height: 1.27m (50in)
Wheelbase: 234cm (92in)
Track: 124cm (48.8in) (front), 127cm (50in) (rear)
Weight: 1156kg (2549lbs)

Bentley 4½ LITRE

Built to be unbreakable, the 4½ Litre thundered around for 24 hours to win Le Mans in 1928 and featured advanced engine technology behind that massive radiator grille.

"...hustled around corners."

"Although the 4½ Litre is heavy, it is also well-balanced and the steering quick and precise. Despite the crude-sounding specification, the Bentley can be hustled around corners quickly and will easily cruise at 145km/h (90mph). The biggest trick to driving it is mastering the non-synchro transmission. Once mastered, however, it's easy to exploit the real power of the Bentley. The weight of the heavy supercharger right at the front turns the 'Blower' Bentley into a determined understeer."

Gauges, gauges everywhere. The Bentley 4½ Litre has gauges for everything set into its beautiful alloy dashboard.

Milestones

1927 Prototype 4½ Litre car appears at the Le Mans 24 Hours but goes out in the infamous White House crash.

1928 4½ Litre wins Le Mans, averaging 111km/h (69mph), despite having no water in the engine at the end.

W. O. Bentley disapproved of supercharging.

1929 4½ Litre of Dunfee/Kidson finishes second at Le Mans behind the winning 6½ Litre Bentley.

1930 First of the supercharged 'Blower' Bentleys is built, a venture by Bentley driver Tim Birkin without W. O. Bentley's support. Engine is redesigned and the supercharger installation is designed by Amherst Villiers.

1932 Tim Birkin's 'Blower' Bentley breaks the outer circuit lap record at Brooklands with a lap at 217km/h (135mph).

Tim Birkin at the wheel of a supercharged 'Blower' Bentley.

UNDER THE SKIN

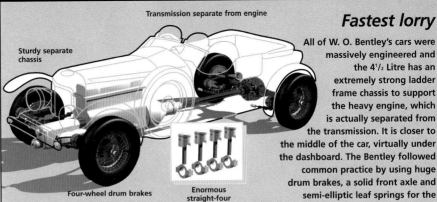

Transmission separate from engine

Sturdy separate chassis

Four-wheel drum brakes

Enormous straight-four

Fastest lorry

All of W. O. Bentley's cars were massively engineered and the 4½ Litre has an extremely strong ladder frame chassis to support the heavy engine, which is actually separated from the transmission. It is closer to the middle of the car, virtually under the dashboard. The Bentley followed common practice by using huge drum brakes, a solid front axle and semi-elliptic leaf springs for the suspension.

THE POWER PACK

Sixteen valve

Although the big four-cylinder is all cast-iron, tall and narrow with a very-long stroke to give a large (although undisclosed) amount of torque, one feature of the 4½ Litre engine still seems modern. It has four valves per cylinder, angled at 30°, and all operated by a single overhead camshaft via a system of rocker arms. The camshaft is driven off the crankshaft via a vertical shaft and bevel gears so there is no chain to break. The 4½ Litre produces 110bhp when naturally aspirated.

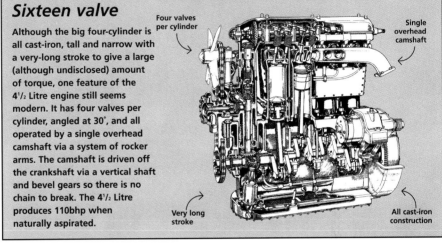

Four valves per cylinder

Single overhead camshaft

Very long stroke

All cast-iron construction

'Blowers'

Although W. O. Bentley vehemently disapproved of supercharging, it's the 54 'Blower' Bentleys which are most famous and desirable, despite their poor competition record. Many Bentley sedans have been converted into 'Blower' replicas.

Supercharged 'Blower' Bentleys are the most desirable of the 4½ Litre cars.

41

Bentley 4½ LITRE

When W. O. Bentley wanted more power from his cars, he made the engines bigger, moving up to 6½ and then 8.0 litres. Ironically the supercharged car he disapproved of so much has become the most famous.

Solid beam front axle

All of W. O. Bentley's cars had a solid beam axle located and sprung by two semi-elliptic leaf springs, along with friction shock absorbers.

Centre lock wheels

Tyre changes could be made quickly in the pits because the Rudge Whitworth wheels have a single knock-off centre fixing, undone with a soft-faced hammer.

Worm-and-wheel steering

The Bentley has a worm-and-wheel. The driver's side wheel is linked to the steering mechanism and a bar from that wheel runs under the chassis to the other front wheel.

Massive brakes

It's heavy and fast, requiring 43.2cm (17in) brakes that are ribbed for cooling. Although Duesenberg had pioneered hydraulic brakes, the Bentley's are cable operated.

Stone guards

The world's race tracks were neither as smooth nor stone-free as today's. To prevent damage, Bentley used stone guards to protect the exposed carburetors next to the supercharger and the fuel tank at the rear.

Fold-down windshield

Although the Bentley had all the aerodynamics of a barn door, the windshield can be folded flat and the small aero-window erected to slightly improve the car's aerodynamics.

External handbrake

There was no room inside the cockpit for the externally mounted handbrake lever. Even the gearshifter isn't in the middle of the cockpit, but off to the driver's side.

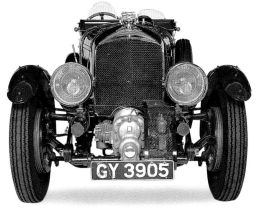

GY 3905

No driver's door

With the side cutaway to allow the driver to move his elbows, there was no need for a door.

GY 3905
GB

Live rear axle

Like all its rivals of the era, the Bentley uses a simple live axle, located and sprung on two semi-elliptic leaf springs.

Specifications

1930 Bentley 4½ Litre supercharged

ENGINE
Type: In-line four cylinder
Construction: Cast-iron block and head
Valve gear: Four valves per cylinder operated by single gear-and shaft-driven overhead camshafts
Bore and stroke: 100mm (3.93in) x 140mm (5.51in)
Displacement: 4398cc (268ci)
Compression ratio: 5.0:1
Induction system: Two SU carburetors with Amherst Villiers Roots-type supercharger
Maximum power: 175bhp at 3500rpm
Maximum power (racing): 240bhp at 2400rpm
Maximum torque: not quoted
Top speed: 201km/h (125mph)
0–96km (0–60mph): not quoted

TRANSMISSION
Four-speed manual

BODY/CHASSIS
Steel ladder frame with cross bracing, and open steel and fabric body

SPECIAL FEATURES

The Roots-type supercharger drives off the crankshaft. Two lobes are rotated, drawing air and fuel through the carburetors, compressing it and forcing it through the intake manifold and into the engine.

RUNNING GEAR
Steering: Worm-and-wheel
Front suspension: Solid beam axle with leaf springs and shocks
Rear suspension: Live axle with semi-elliptic leaf springs and shocks
Brakes: Four-wheel drums
Wheels: Rudge Whitworth 15.24cm (6in) x 50.8cm (20in)
Tyres: Dunlop crossply, 15.24cm (6in) x 50.8cm (20in)

DIMENSIONS
Length: 4.38m (172.5in)
Width: 1.74m (68.5in)
Height: 1.6m (63in)
Wheelbase: 330cm (130in)
Track: 138cm (54.49in) (front and rear)
Weight: 1921kg (4235lbs)

Bentley **CONTINENTAL R**

In the early 1950s, the Continental must have seemed like a vision from another world. It was a Bentley that remained true to the company ideals of sporty driving reserved for the more affluent enthusiast. It remains one of the most beautiful cars of all time.

"...profoundly impressive."

"Even today, the experience of driving a Continental R is profoundly impressive. From the moment you step into the cockpit, with its tailored leather seats and rich wood ambience, you know you're in for a treat. You sit up high with a fabulous view over the long bonnet. The engine likes to be pressed hard and delivers a fair turn of speed with an impressive silence. The shifter has a smooth, well-oiled action that betrays the high-quality engineering behind it."

Despite the austerity of the period, the Bentley has an incredibly luxurious interior.

Milestones

1950 Rolls-Royce signals the go-ahead for a fast touring Bentley model and asks coachbuilder H.J. Mulliner to build the prototype (nicknamed 'Olga') on the Bentley Mk VI sedan chassis.

Italian styling house Pininfarina also bodied Continental Rs.

1952 At the London Motor Show, the Continental R enraptures press and public alike.

1954 A larger 4.9-litre engine becomes standard and an automatic transmission is offered as an option.

A new Continental R debuted as the 1990s unfolded.

1955 Production is suspended as the model is replaced by a new Bentley S1-based Continental coupé.

UNDER THE SKIN

Aerodynamic bodywork

Live rear axle

Independent front suspension

Inlet-over-exhaust six

Best in the world

The Continental owes its underpinnings to the Bentley Mark VI sedan. The independent front suspension is by wishbones and coilsprings, the upper wishbones being formed by the lever-armshock absorbers with leaf springs at the rear. The cam-and-peg steering is unassisted, but there is servo assistance for the brakes.

THE POWER PACK

Whispering power

Until the advent of V8 engines in 1959, all Bentley and Rolls-Royce engines were developments of the company's well-tried straight-six engine. By 1952, this was a sizable 4.6-litre unit, with the intake valves overhead and the exhaust valves mounted to the side. Rolls-Royce never published official power outputs – it merely described output as adequate. We now know that this meant around 150bhp, rising to approximately 175bhp with the 4.9-litre engine. Torque for the 4.6-litre engine is estimated at 147lb-ft.

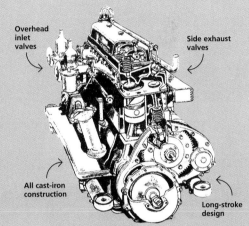

Overhead inlet valves

Side exhaust valves

All cast-iron construction

Long-stroke design

Classic style

Of all postwar Bentleys, the Continental R is the most coveted. Its body is among the most handsome of all automobiles and its rarity adds to the mystique. The original Continental has a style and class that later cars with the same name never seemed to match.

The Continental R has handsome fastback styling.

Bentley CONTINENTAL R

This was the world's most expensive car in 1952, and was also a strong contender as the world's fastest four-seater road car. This pinnacle of the touring car tradition was also one of the most handsome cars ever made.

Straight-six engine

The intake-over-exhaust straight-six engine could easily get the hefty Continental R moving along at more than 160km/h (100mph).

Choice of transmission

The four-speed manual transmission was a model of slick operation and has a higher final drive ratio for relaxed high-speed cruising. A four-speed automatic transmission was also available.

Classic Bentley grille

To distinguish Bentley from Rolls-Royce, the grille is very different. The profile is more rounded and the 'Flying Lady' mascot is replaced by Bentley's winged 'B'. In the interest of cutting frontal area, and hence drag, the height of the grille is reduced by 3.8cm (1.5in).

Comfortable suspension

To achieve the optimum ride quality, there is an independent coil-sprung wishbone front end and a semi-elliptic leaf-sprung rear axle.

Elegant coachwork

To true automotive enthusiasts, the Continental R remains one of the greatest all-time body designs. The aluminium body was hand-crafted by H.J. Mulliner.

Aerodynamic shape

The body was shaped by the wind, literally, as it was developed in the Rolls-Royce wind tunnel. The fastback shape certainly helped airflow, as did the curved windshield. An uncanny lack of wind noise was one important fringe benefit.

Sporty interior

The Continental has a wooden dashboard, deep-pile carpeting, front bucket seats and leather upholstery. The prominent tachometer's redline is set at 4250rpm.

Specifications

1952 Bentley Continental R

ENGINE

Type: In-line six-cylinder

Construction: Cast-iron block and aluminium head

Valve gear: Two valves per cylinder, (overhead inlet/side exhaust) operated by a single camshaft via pushrods and rockers

Bore and stroke: 92mm (3.62in) x 114mm (4.50in)

Displacement: 4566cc (279ci)

Compression ratio: 7.0:1

Induction system: Two SU carburetors

Maximum power: Not quoted

Maximum torque: Not quoted

Top speed: 188km/h (117mph)

0–96km (0–60mph): 13.5 sec

TRANSMISSION

Four-speed manual

BODY/CHASSIS

Separate chassis with aluminium two-door coupé body

SPECIAL FEATURES

The high-quality engineering even extends to the alloy gas filler cap.

The lowered radiator grille carries the traditional Bentley winged 'B' mascot.

RUNNING GEAR

Steering: Cam-and-roller

Front suspension: Wishbones with coil springs and lever-arm shock absorbers

Rear suspension: Live axle with semi-elliptic leaf springs and adjustable telescopic shock absorbers

Brakes: Drums (front and rear)

Wheels: Steel, 40.6cm (16in) dia.

Tyres: 6.50 x 16

DIMENSIONS

Length: 5.24m (206.4in)

Width: 1.82m (71.5in)

Height: 1.6m (63.0in)

Wheelbase: 305cm (120.0in)

Track: 144cm (256.7in) (front), 149cm (58.5in) (rear)

Weight: 1607kg (3543lbs)

Bentley **TURBO R/T**

W. O. Bentley would have approved of the Turbo R/T – a big, powerful and fast sedan – as much as he did of the fabled sports and luxury cars he built during the 1920s.

"...Appearance is deceiving"

"Appearances can be deceiving, as the Turbo R/T demonstrates. With its chubby exterior, you would expect it to be more of a land yacht than a sports car, yet it performs magnificently. The chassis is agile thanks to very stiff springs and electronic shocks. Its massive turbocharged V8 gives awesome results. It's hard to believe that this hulk will hit 96km/h (60mph) from a rest in just 6.7 seconds."

The interior has all the class and luxury of an old-fashioned gentleman's club, with wood and leather everywhere.

Milestones

1965 The first 'modern' Bentley,
the T1, is launched. It is the company's first monocoque car.

Bentley's original Turbo R was based on the 1985 Rolls Royce.

1980 The new Mulsanne is launched.
It uses the Rolls-Royce Silver Spirit bodyshell.

1982 Bentley turbocharges the
Mulsanne, giving an enormous (but undisclosed) power output.

The Turbo R/T uses the engine from the elegant Continental T.

1985 The Turbo R is launched.
It produces 320bhp and 457lb-ft of torque.

1997 Bentley introduces the Turbo R/T,
which uses a 400-bhp version of the Continental T engine.

UNDER THE SKIN

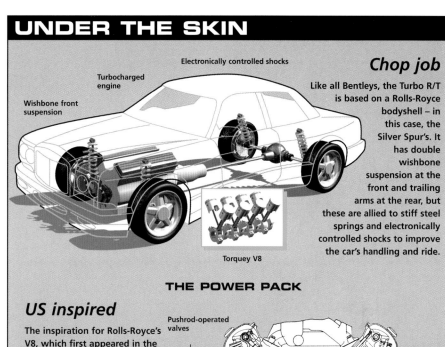

Electronically controlled shocks

Turbocharged engine

Wishbone front suspension

Torquey V8

Chop job

Like all Bentleys, the Turbo R/T is based on a Rolls-Royce bodyshell – in this case, the Silver Spur's. It has double wishbone suspension at the front and trailing arms at the rear, but these are allied to stiff steel springs and electronically controlled shocks to improve the car's handling and ride.

THE POWER PACK

US inspired

The inspiration for Rolls-Royce's V8, which first appeared in the late 1950s, came from the US. It follows the same principles of a large displacement engine (nearly 7.0 litres) and a single central camshaft and two valves per cylinder. Unlike most traditional large American V8s, it is made of alloy and not cast iron, with wet liners. In the Turbo R/T, it is fitted with a Garrett turbocharger to give masses of power output and impressive torque at just 2000rpm.

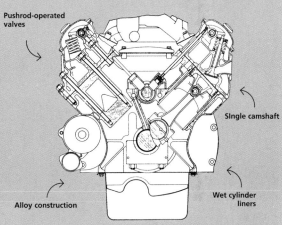

Pushrod-operated valves

Single camshaft

Wet cylinder liners

Alloy construction

Throwback

Although W.O. Bentley was always opposed to forced induction engines, the turbocharged Bentleys – the Turbo R and Turbo R/T – have recaptured the spirit of the company's sportier cars of the 1930s. There are few modern cars that can boast such a high power output.

Bentley's Turbo R/T is big on performance and, of course, style.

Bentley TURBO R/T

The Bentley Turbo R/T is an enormous car with a huge power output and almost excessive luxury. Unsurprisingly, it has an enormous price tag to match.

Electronic shocks

The key to the Bentley's great poise is its electronic shocks. Each shock is adjusted in microseconds to cope with the changes in road surface and speed or cornering forces.

Turbo V8 engine

The naturally aspirated Rolls/Bentley V8 produces enough power, but to increase the output to 400bhp the engine is now turbocharged. More important for performance is the increase in torque that turbocharging produces.

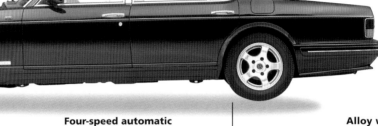

Four-speed automatic

The four-speed automatic transmission has adaptive changes – it learns the driver's style whether relaxed or enthusiastic, and varies the shift points accordingly.

Alloy wheels

To carry the Bentley's great weight and handle the performance, the Turbo R/T needs large wheels and is fitted with handsome and wide five-spoke alloys.

Semi-trailing arm rear suspension

Semi-trailing arm rear suspension has been used on Rolls-Royces and Bentleys for many years. It's retained on the the Turbo R/T, but with much of the compliance engineered out.

Connolly leather interior

The interior is covered in Connolly leather, including the seats, steering wheel, gear selector, door panels and windshield pillars.

Specifications

1998 Bentley Turbo R/T

ENGINE

Type: V8

Construction: Alloy block and heads

Valve gear: Two valves per cylinder operated by single camshafts via pushrods

Bore and stroke: 104mm (4.09in) x 99mm (3.89in)

Displacement: 6750cc (412ci)

Compression ratio: 8.0:1

Induction system: Zytec EMS3 controlled electronic fuel injection with Garrett T04B turbocharger

Maximum power: 400bhp at 4000rpm

Maximum torque: 490lb-ft at 2000rpm

Top speed: 245km/h (152mph)

0–96km (0–60mph): 6.7 sec

TRANSMISSION

Four-speed automatic

BODY/CHASSIS

Monocoque four-door saloon

SPECIAL FEATURES

The sportier Bentleys have mesh radiator grilles rather than the chrome ones used on Rolls-Royces.

RUNNING GEAR

Steering: Rack-and-pinion

Front suspension: Double wishbones with coil springs, electronically controlled shocks and anti-roll bar

Rear suspension: Semi-trailing arms, coil springs, electronically controlled shocks and anti-roll bar

Brakes: Vented discs (front), solid discs (rear); ABS standard

Wheels: Alloy, 21.6cm (8.5in) x 45.7cm (18in)

Tyres: 265/45 ZR18

DIMENSIONS

Length: 5.4m (212.4in)

Width: 2.1m (83.1in)

Height: 1.49m (58.5in)

Wheelbase: 316cm (124.5in)

Track: 155cm (61in) (front and rear)

Weight: 2472kg (5450lbs)

Bristol **407/411**

In 1947, Bristol diversified from making airplanes into building specialist upscale cars. These were known for their fine workmanship and sports-car handling. The V8-engined cars introduced another feature – performance.

"...high level of refinement."

"Even today, the Bristol is an amazingly effortless car to drive, with its torquey V8 pulling smoothly from very low revs and the TorqueFlite automatic transmission providing seamless shifts. The car is at its best cruising at high speed or on long, sweeping out-of-town roads. Where it seems to break away from the pavement is around tight corners. The steering feels vague and becomes heavy at lower speeds, yet the high level of refinement and ride compensate."

Typical of a 1960s British car, the 407 has plenty of walnut and leather upholstery.

Milestones

1961 Bristol replaces its six-cylinder 406
model with the V8-powered 407. Soon after, ownership of the company passes from Bristol Aircraft to racing driver Anthony Crook and Sir George White.

A very special Bristol was the 1960–1961 406 with stunning coachwork by Zagato.

1963 407 production comes
to an end as the new 408, with its restyled bodywork, enters the arena.

The 409 gained better Girling disc brakes.

1965 Looking almost
identical to the 408, a new model, the 409, supersedes it. It has a larger Chrysler V8 but similar power.

1968 More chrome and smaller
wheels identify the new 410.

1969 The 411 gains a bigger
engine with 335bhp. It lasts until 1976.

UNDER THE SKIN

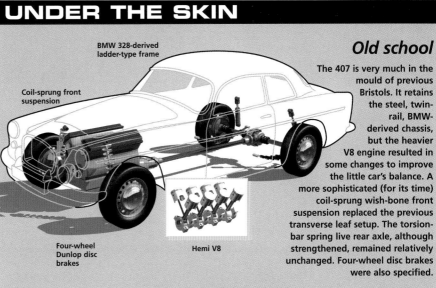

BMW 328-derived ladder-type frame

Coil-sprung front suspension

Four-wheel Dunlop disc brakes

Hemi V8

Old school

The 407 is very much in the mould of previous Bristols. It retains the steel, twin-rail, BMW-derived chassis, but the heavier V8 engine resulted in some changes to improve the little car's balance. A more sophisticated (for its time) coil-sprung wish-bone front suspension replaced the previous transverse leaf setup. The torsion-bar spring live rear axle, although strengthened, remained relatively unchanged. Four-wheel disc brakes were also specified.

THE POWER PACK

Chrysler Hemi V8

Until the 407, Bristol cars had always been powered by a known winner – the BMW-derived six-cylinder. In 1961, the company had to face the challenge of rising horse-power wars with its competitors. Bristol decided to go down the V8 route – and never looked back. The natural selection was a Chrysler of Canada-produced 5129cc (313ci) Hemi engine that was built specially to Bristol's requirements. With solid lifters, a higher-lift camshaft and a Carter four-barrel carburetor, the 407 has a quoted power output of 250bhp.

V8 milestone

As the first of the V8-powered Bristols, the 407 is historic in its way. It is faster than previous cars, though slightly less nimble through corners. All 407s were built as two-door coupés and, interestingly, most 407s were exported to the U.S.

The introduction of the 407 marked a new era for Bristol.

Bristol 407/411

Bristols are unique: conservative in style, advanced in features, luxurious yet sporty in character and always more exclusive than Rolls-Royce. The V8 407 marked a new departure, but it still had top-notch quality.

V8 power

For the first time, Bristol used V8 engines in its 407 instead of straight sixes. The engine came from Chrysler in Canada and was modified by Bristol to extract greater power and make it more free-revving.

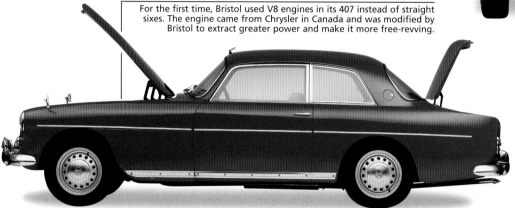

Four-wheel disc brakes

Disc brakes are necessary to stop the considerable bulk of the 407. Bristol specified substantial 27.9cm (11in) Dunlop discs on all four wheels.

Pre-war chassis

The bulky separate chassis under the 407 dated from the prewar era, being a direct development of the BMW 326 chassis. Remarkably, this chassis is still in use in Bristol's current car, the Blenheim.

Luxurious cabin

The dashboard is fine walnut veneer, and there is full leather upholstery and rich carpeting. All the instruments (a total of seven) are grouped together in an easy-to-see cluster directly in front of the driver. The only option was an HMV radio and two speakers.

Ample interior space

Compared to most other sporty luxury cars of its era, the Bristol boasts plenty of space for four 1.8-m (6-ft) tall passengers. Enormous armchair-like front seats can recline for comfort and have built-in headrests.

Aluminium bodywork

Aluminium was more abundant than steel in post-war Europe. Bristol was originally an airplane manufacturer and knew the benefits of aluminium: although it was more expensive than steel, it was lighter, easier to hand-form and entirely impervious to rust.

Aircraft-inspired nose

The 407 was the last Bristol to have this distinctive nose treatment, which is strongly reminiscent of airplanes. The front grille is set in to force cool air into the engine bay.

Specifications

1962 Bristol 407

ENGINE

Type: V8

Construction: Cast-iron block and heads

Valve gear: Two valves per cylinder operated by a single camshaft

Bore and stroke: 98mm (3.86in) x 84mm (3.31in)

Displacement: 5130cc (313ci)

Compression ratio: 9.0:1

Induction system: Carter four-barrel carburetor

Maximum power: 250bhp at 4400rpm

Maximum torque: 340lb-ft at 2800rpm

Top speed: 196km/h (122mph)

0–96km (0–60mph): 9.9 sec

TRANSMISSION

TorqueFlite three-speed automatic

BODY/CHASSIS

Separate chassis with aluminium two-door sedan body

SPECIAL FEATURES

Like Chryslers of the period, the 407 has push-button transmission controls.

RUNNING GEAR

Steering: Cam-and-roller

Front suspension: Unequal-length wishbones with coil springs, shock absorbers and anti-roll bar

Rear suspension: Live axle with Watt linkage, shock absorbers and longitudinal torsion bars

Brakes: Discs (front and rear)

Wheels: Steel discs, 40.6cm (16in) dia.

Tyres: Dunlop, 6.00 x H16

DIMENSIONS

Length: 5m (199.0in)

Width: 1.7m (68.0in)

Height: 1.5m (60.0in)

Wheelbase: 290cm (114.0in)

Track: 135cm (53.0in) (front), 138cm (54.5in) (rear)

Weight: 1651kg (3640lbs)

Caterham **SUPER 7**

When Colin Chapman became tired of the Lotus Seven and decided that it had no future with the company, Caterham Cars took over production. Over the years, Caterham has consistently improved the car, turning the Super Seven into a world beater.

"...a road-going racing car."

"It is just about the nearest thing to a road-going racing car that you'll find. With its extraordinary acceleration, handling and braking, just a touch of the steering wheel is needed to point the Seven in the direction you want to go, and it sticks to the road like glue. The bone-shaking ride, the exhilaration of the wind howling past the flat windshield and the deafening noise of the engine all remind you that this is a traditional sports car."

The cockpit is strictly functional, and the small steering wheel gives an instant response.

Milestones

1957 The Lotus Seven S1, designed by Colin Chapman, makes its first appearance with wishbone front suspension, live rear axle and an 1172cc (72ci) Ford engine.

Many Lotus and Caterham Sevens have bare aluminium bodywork.

1973 Caterham cars

takes over production of the Lotus Seven and produces the S3 model.

1985 A superior de Dion

rear suspension is introduced to supplement the existing live-axle arrangement.

The JPE was specially created to win a 0–100–0mph challenge set by a British magazine.

1991 Caterham fits the

1.4-litre Rover K-series engine to the Seven.

1997 New variants

of the Seven keep appearing. The ultimate development for 1997 is the 187bhp Superlight R.

UNDER THE SKIN

De Dion rear suspension

Tubular steel spaceframe chassis

Four-wheel disc brakes

Wishbone front suspension

Vauxhall four-cylinder

Proven design

Like the original Super Seven, the Caterham car has a steel tube spaceframe chassis, but this is stronger and stiffer. Steel tubes run lengthwise over the driveshaft, effectively forming a centre backbone. The sides of the chassis are paneled with aluminium sheets. The network of small diameter steel tubes holds the front and rear suspension.

THE POWER PACK

Off-the-shelf engine

Caterham Sevens have used many different engines from a number of manufacturers such as Ford and Rover. This HPC unit is a Vauxhall four-cylinder with an iron block and alloy 16-valve head with twin overhead camshafts. It revs willingly, right up to the 7800rpm redline, and yet uses adjustment-free hydraulic lifters. Although fuel-injected in its Vauxhall form, Caterham adds large, twin 45-mm (1.8in) Weber carburetors, which allow the engine to produce 175bhp. Torque is rated at an impressive 155lb-ft.

Adjustment-free hydraulic lifters

Twin overhead camshafts

Cast-iron cylinder block

Free-flow exhaust system

Power crazy

One of the fastest production Caterham Sevens is the HPC. Powered by a 175bhp, 2.0-litre Vauxhall engine, it can reach 96km/h (60mph) in under six seconds. The current equivalent is the Superlight R with a 187bhp Rover power unit.

In 1992, the top Super Seven is the HPC with a 2.0-litre Vauxhall engine.

Caterham SUPER 7

The Caterham Super Seven, with its sheer excitement, immediate response and driver involvement, is arguably more like a four-wheeled motorbike than a conventional car.

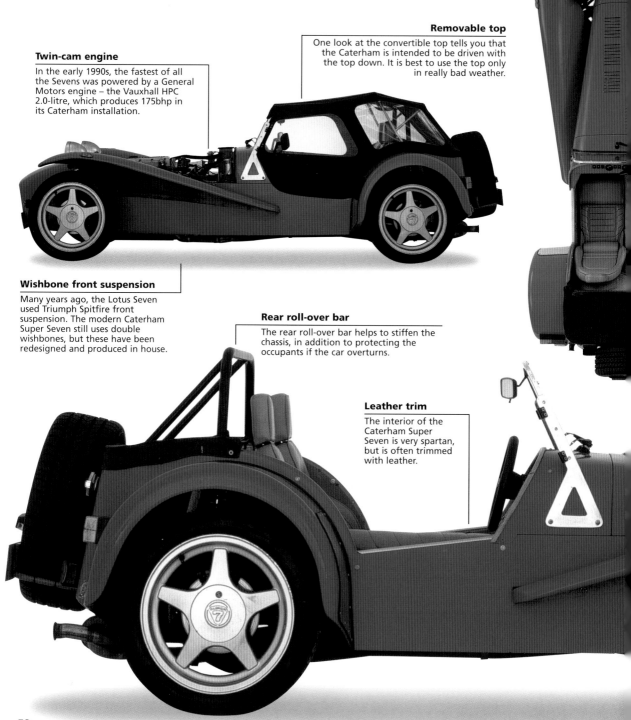

Twin-cam engine

In the early 1990s, the fastest of all the Sevens was powered by a General Motors engine – the Vauxhall HPC 2.0-litre, which produces 175bhp in its Caterham installation.

Removable top

One look at the convertible top tells you that the Caterham is intended to be driven with the top down. It is best to use the top only in really bad weather.

Wishbone front suspension

Many years ago, the Lotus Seven used Triumph Spitfire front suspension. The modern Caterham Super Seven still uses double wishbones, but these have been redesigned and produced in house.

Rear roll-over bar

The rear roll-over bar helps to stiffen the chassis, in addition to protecting the occupants if the car overturns.

Leather trim

The interior of the Caterham Super Seven is very spartan, but is often trimmed with leather.

Low-profile tyres

The 1990s Caterhams run on low-profile Goodyear Eagles – tyres that had not even been dreamt of when the original Lotus Seven was developed.

Ford Sierra transmission

The five-speed transmission supplied by Ford is the same as that used in the British Ford Sierra. In the Super Seven, it is mounted on Caterham's own bellhousing to mate it to the Vauxhall engine.

Specifications

1992 Caterham Super Seven HPC

ENGINE
Type: Vauxhall in-line four-cylinder
Construction: Cast-iron block and alloy cylinder head
Valve gear: Two valves per cylinder operated by twin overhead camshafts via hydraulic lifters
Bore and stroke: 86mm (3.38in) x 86mm (3.38in)
Displacement: 1998cc (122ci)
Compression ratio: 10.5:1
Induction system: Two Weber 45 DCOE sidedraft carburetors
Maximum power: 175bhp at 6000rpm
Maximum torque: 155lb-ft at 4800rpm
Top speed: 203km/h (126mph)
0–96km (0–60mph): 5.4 sec

TRANSMISSION
Ford five-speed manual

BODY/CHASSIS
Tubular steel spaceframe with aluminium honeycomb, alloy sheet and fibreglass bodywork

SPECIAL FEATURES
Caterham Cars has stiffened the steel spaceframe chassis to further improve handling.

RUNNING GEAR
Steering: Rack-and-pinion
Front suspension: Double wishbones with coil springs, telescopic shocks and anti-roll bars
Rear suspension: De Dion axle with coil springs, telescopic shocks and anti-roll bar
Brakes: Four-wheel discs, 22.9cm (9in) dia.
Wheels: Alloy, 17.8cm (7in) x 40.6cm (16in)
Tyres: Goodyear Eagle NCT 205/45 VR16

DIMENSIONS
Length: 3.4m (133.5in)
Width: 1.6m (61.8in)
Height: 1.07m (42.5in)
Wheelbase: 222.8cm (87.8in)
Track: 124cm (48.8in) (front), 133cm (52.5in) (rear)
Weight: 628kg (1385lbs)

Dare **DZ**

The ranks of British sports cars have been joined by a new name, Dare. The DZ is a lightweight, mid-engined road rocket that concentrates on handling and performance. It looks as wild as it is fast.

"...sports car heaven."

"Getting into the gullwing DZ is a challenge, as you climb over the wide rocker panels and into the very narrow seats. Once in place, you're in sports car heaven, with a great driving position and a front-row view of the suspension in action. It's very quick off the line and boasts instant cornering response with little body roll and finely weighted steering. The ride quality is superb, while the high-specification brakes do a fantastic job of stopping the car."

Unlike the stripped-out cabins of some of its rivals, the DZ has a fully trimmed interior.

Milestones

1991 The two Walklett brothers

who originally founded the Ginetta company in 1957, form Dare to make updated versions of historic Ginetta designs.

One of Ginetta's later creations was the G32, derived from Ford Fiesta running gear.

1998 At the Birmingham Motor

Show in the UK, the all-new Dare DZ model is presented in coupé and roadster forms.

Ford's new Focus uses the same 2-litre engine as the Dare, but it is nearly twice the DZ's weight.

1999 Automobile magazines get their

hands on the new cars and are full of praise for the Dare's uncompromising character, refined but stunning performance and originality. Production continues in Colchester.

UNDER THE SKIN

Race car ideals

The engineers behind the DZ have a distinguished competition career, and it shows. The bonded steel and composite chassis/tub is as light as possible, and the running gear components are designed and manufactured exclusively for the DZ. The front suspension mimics Grand Prix racers; aerodynamic wishbones and inboard coil/spring shock units. The rear suspension is a state-of-the-art double wishbone setup.

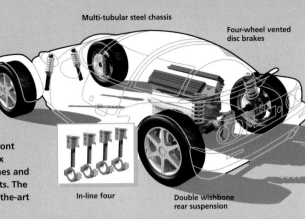

Multi-tubular steel chassis

Four-wheel vented disc brakes

In-line four

Double wishbone rear suspension

THE POWER PACK

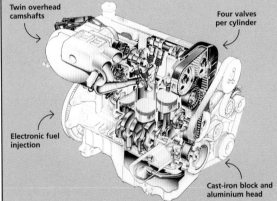

Twin overhead camshafts

Four valves per cylinder

Electronic fuel injection

Cast-iron block and aluminium head

Ford Zetec

The ultimate in handling comes from cars with mid-mounted engines, and the Dare is no exception. In entry-level form, the powerplant is a transversely mounted Ford 2.0-litre Zetec unit with 130bhp. But for truly outrageous performance, the company offers a specially developed supercharged version with more than 50 perc ent extra power – no less than 210bhp at 6000rpm. In a car weighing so little, this is a huge amount of power – equivalent to 308bhp per ton.

DZ convertible

Of the two body styles, the convertible is the better choice simply because it's more fun and maintains the minimalist spirit of the car. If you really want a thrill, try out the speedy 210bhp supercharged version – you won't believe how much power it produces.

The supercharged DZ reaches 96km/h (60mph) in just 4.7 seconds.

Dare DZ

No other car looks like the DZ, but its race car-inspired mechanical specification does not prevent it from being surprisingly practical and comfortable to drive.

Luxurious interior

The Dare's interior is designed to be as comfortable as possible. The seating is in full leather, with a neat 'Dare' badge embroidered in the headrests, and there's full carpeting and a smart aluminium kickplate on the floor. Emphasizing the racing pedigree, there are four-point harnesses for the driver and the passenger.

Tough chassis

Most of the strength of the chassis is in the central tub, which is made from composite material with bonded steel tubing on the floor, just under the doors and below the windshield. Steel box sections front and rear carry the suspension and engine.

Supercharged option

Although this car is fitted with a normally aspirated engine, the star choice is a specially developed supercharged unit. Based on the 2.0-litre Ford Zetec four-cylinder, it has 210bhp, enough to push the DZ from 0–96km/h (0–60mph) in 4.7 seconds.

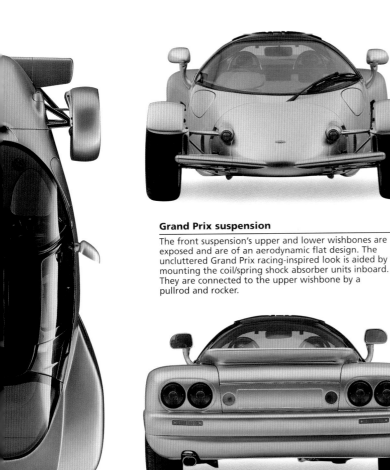

Grand Prix suspension

The front suspension's upper and lower wishbones are exposed and are of an aerodynamic flat design. The uncluttered Grand Prix racing-inspired look is aided by mounting the coil/spring shock absorber units inboard. They are connected to the upper wishbone by a pullrod and rocker.

Unusual styling

The DZ originated as a showpiece for the design consultancy talents of the Walklett brothers. Highly individual, it has a very low, narrow nose leading to a high and wide tail section. The car is extremely compact, measuring just over 3.45m (136in).

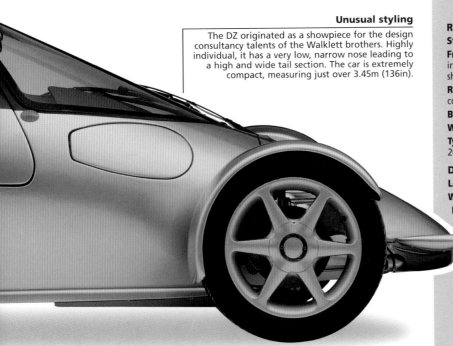

Specifications

1998 Dare DZ

ENGINE

Type: In-line four-cylinder

Construction: Cast-iron block and aluminium cylinder head

Valve gear: Four valves per cylinder operated by twin overhead camshafts

Bore and stroke: 85mm (3.34in) x 88mm (3.46in)

Displacement: 1988cc (122ci)

Compression ratio: 10.0:1

Induction system: Ford EFI

Maximum power: 130bhp at 5750rpm

Maximum torque: 129lb-ft at 3700rpm

Top speed: 209km/h (130mph)

0–96km (0–60mph): 5.8 sec

TRANSMISSION

Five-speed manual

BODY/CHASSIS

Composite and multi-tubular steel monocoque chassis with fibreglass two-door coupé or roadster body

SPECIAL FEATURES

For a smooth profile, the headlights are sited in pods that pivot into the body.

RUNNING GEAR

Steering: Rack-and-pinion

Front suspension: Double wishbones with inboard coil springs, pullrods, rockers, shock absorbers and anti-roll bar

Rear suspension: Double wishbones with coil springs and shock absorbers

Brakes: Vented discs (front and rear)

Wheels: Alloy, 38.1cm (15in) dia.

Tyres: 195/50 15 (front), 205/50 15 (rear)

DIMENSIONS

Length: 3.46m (136.6in)

Width: 1.65m (65.0in)

Height: 1m (40.5in)

Wheelbase: 224cm (88.0in)

Track: 145cm (57.0in) (front and rear)

Weight: 680kg (1500lbs)

Jaguar **XK120**

In a world where other manufacturers were still recycling old prewar designs, Jaguar came up with a complete contrast; the XK120 was sleek, fast, modern – and also incredibly cheap.

"...wonderful, smooth straight-six."

"It doesn't take long to see why the XK120 would have been astonishing in 1948. There's masses of power and torque from that wonderful, smooth straight-six, and the performance is incredible. It's easy to drive too; that big steering wheel set close to your chest is necessary at slow speeds, but the steering lightens up as speed rises. The crossply tyres don't generate very much grip but are more progressive in their behaviour than modern radials."

Although more sporty than Fixed Head or Drophead Coupés, the Roadster's interior was still luxurious by any standard.

Milestones

1940 Streamlined BMW 328 wins the Mille Miglia. The styling influences William Lyons when he comes to design the XK120.

The C-type was the successful racing version of the XK120.

1948 XK120 Roadster is launched at the British Motor Show and called the Open Two Seater Super Sports. True convertibles and hardtop coupé models soon follow.

1950 An XK120 wins the Tourist Trophy race and comes close to victory at the 24 Hours of Le Mans.

The last of the XK line is the 3.4-litre XK150 of 1957.

1952 A coupé version is driven round the banked circuit of Montlhery near Paris for a whole week at an average of more than 160km/h (100mph).

1953 Jaguar takes an XK120 to the long straight Jabbeke motorway in Belgium and achieves a high speed of more than 274kmn/h (170mph).

1954 Production ends after 12,000 cars are built.

UNDER THE SKIN

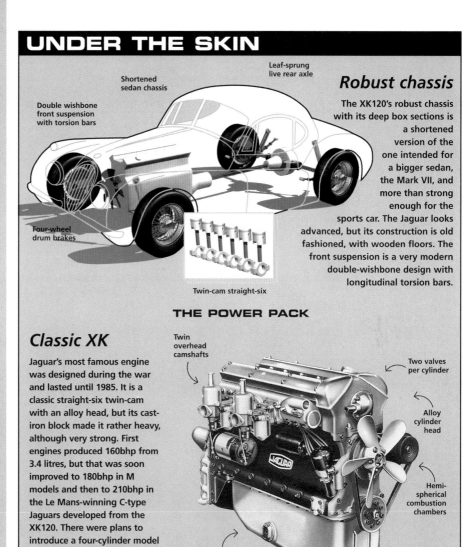

Leaf-sprung live rear axle

Shortened sedan chassis

Double wishbone front suspension with torsion bars

Four-wheel drum brakes

Twin-cam straight-six

Robust chassis

The XK120's robust chassis with its deep box sections is a shortened version of the one intended for a bigger sedan, the Mark VII, and more than strong enough for the sports car. The Jaguar looks advanced, but its construction is old fashioned, with wooden floors. The front suspension is a very modern double-wishbone design with longitudinal torsion bars.

THE POWER PACK

Classic XK

Jaguar's most famous engine was designed during the war and lasted until 1985. It is a classic straight-six twin-cam with an alloy head, but its cast-iron block made it rather heavy, although very strong. First engines produced 160bhp from 3.4 litres, but that was soon improved to 180bhp in M models and then to 210bhp in the Le Mans-winning C-type Jaguars developed from the XK120. There were plans to introduce a four-cylinder model with a cut-down version of the XK engine.

Twin overhead camshafts

Two valves per cylinder

Alloy cylinder head

Hemi-spherical combustion chambers

Cast-iron block

Early alloy

Rarest of all the XK120s are the first 240 cars, all Roadsters, which have bodies hand-formed in aluminium. When demand for the XK120 took off, the cars were made with steel bodywork and are about 50kg (110lbs) heavier than the earlier cars.

Early, alloy-bodied XK120s are lightweight and very rare.

Jaguar **XK120**

Where the prewar Jaguar SS100 had been the absolutely typical 1930s sports car, the XK120 looked to the future. It was in a class of its own because none of its rivals could come close in looks or performance.

Wishbone front suspension

Engine apart, the XK120's most advanced feature is its double-wishbone front suspension with torsion bars and telescopic shock absorbers instead of lever arm devices.

Twin-cam engine

The XK twin-cam six, which started life in the XK120, went on to power the C- and D-type racers, the XK140 and XK150, and the Jaguar sedans up to and beyond the XJ6.

Fitted rear luggage

To make the best possible use of the Jaguar's boot space, fitted luggage was an option.

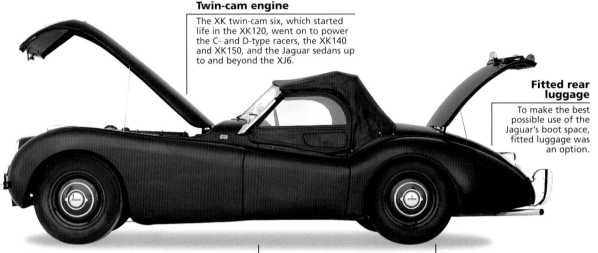

Alloy bodywork

Very early XK120s have all aluminium-alloy bodywork, joined to the chassis in 12 places. The alloy panels were soon replaced by steel.

Live rear axle

The XK120 uses a traditional live axle located and sprung on semi-elliptic leaf springs with lever arm shocks.

Connolly leather seats

On the cars fitted with leather trim, high-quality Connolly leather is used for the seats and the trim around the doors.

Rear wheel skirts

The removable wheel skirts are for style and aerodynamic efficiency, but they can be fitted with steel disc wheels only, because the spinners on the wire wheels project too far.

No rear bumper

To begin with, only these small rear over-riders were fitted, but later XK models grew larger and larger bumpers.

Removable windshield

On the roadster, the windshield can be completely removed if you really want wind-in-the-hair motoring. The windshield pillars unbolt from the bodywork. On the coupé and convertible model, the windshield pillars are part of the bodywork.

Specifications
1951 Jaguar XK120 M

ENGINE
Type: In-line six
Construction: Cast-iron block, aluminum alloy cylinder head
Valve gear: Two valves per cylinder operated by twin overhead camshafts
Bore and stroke: 83mm (3.26in) x 106mm (4.17in)
Displacement: 3442cc (210ci)
Compression ratio: 8.0:1
Induction system: Two SU H6 carburetors
Maximum power: 180bhp at 5300rpm
Maximum torque: 203lb-ft at 4000rpm
Top Speed: 193km/h (120mph)
0–96km/h (0–60mph): 10 seconds

TRANSMISSION
Four-speed manual

BODY/CHASSIS
Separate box section chassis with steel open-roadster body

SPECIAL FEATURES

XK120's curvaceous and wind-cheating lines were a revelation in 1948.

RUNNING GEAR
Steering: Recirculating ball
Front suspension: Double wishbones with longitudinal torsion bars and telescopic shocks
Rear suspension: Live axle with semi-elliptic leaf springs and lever arm shocks
Brakes: Drums (front and rear)
Wheels: Steel disc or wire spoke, 40.6cm (16in) dia.
Tyres: Crossply 15.2cm (6in) x 40.6cm (16in)

DIMENSIONS
Length: 4.4m (174in)
Width: 1.57m (62in)
Height: 1.35m (53in)
Wheelbase: 259cm (102in)
Track: 129.5cm (51in) (front), 127cm (50in) (rear)
Weight: 1378kg (3039lbs)

Jaguar **D-TYPE**

Jaguar designed the D-type with one aim in mind – to create a car that could win the most important race in the world, the 24 Hours of Le Mans. It achieved three straight victories in the mid-1950s.

"...tractable in traffic."

"By any standards, the D-type is an astonishing car with straight-line power to frighten many current supercars. A lack of cockpit space is emphasized by the big central rib, and the steering wheel feels big and skinny. The gearshift is positive, but heavy. None of the other controls are unduly heavy. Surprisingly for a race car, the D-type is tractable in traffic. But find an open road and it rockets to 96km/h (60mph) in just over 5 seconds and tops 261km/h (162mph)."

A bulky transmission tunnel results in a snug fit inside the cockpit.

Milestones

1953 Jaguar's XK120C Mk 2 is first seen in October, when it reaches nearly 290km/h (180mph) on a closed Belgian motorway.

The C-type started Jaguar's run of success at Le Mans.

1954 Now known as the D-type, three cars are entered in the 24 Hours of Le Mans. Two drop out, but the third car takes second place.

1955 Fitted with longer noses, two D-types take first and third at Le Mans.

Jaguar's next specialist racer was the lightweight E-type.

1956 An Ecurie Ecosse D-type wins at Le Mans, with a poor showing from the works cars.

1957 Jaguar no longer campaigns the D-type, but an Ecurie Ecosse car wins Le Mans again. New regulations result in the D-type's demise.

UNDER THE SKIN

Proven and new

The D-type's chassis owes as much to aircraft-industry thinking as to conventional race-car engineering. Whereas most racing sports cars in the mid-1950s still relied on a ladder-type frame, or at best a tubular spaceframe, the D-type uses a strong central monocoque with a separate subframe to support the engine and front suspension. Like its predecessor, the D-type has a live rear axle and four-wheel disc brakes.

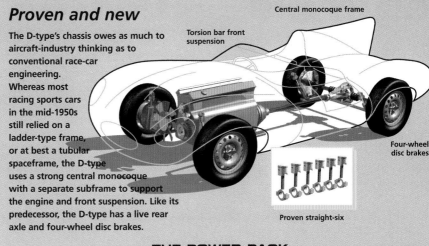

Central monocoque frame

Torsion bar front suspension

Four-wheel disc brakes

Proven straight-six

THE POWER PACK

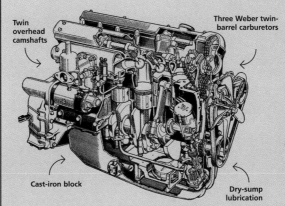

Twin overhead camshafts

Three Weber twin-barrel carburetors

Cast-iron block

Dry-sump lubrication

Unstopable XK

The D-type uses a 3442cc (210ci) version of Jaguar's famous twin-cam XK engine. It is derived from the C-type's iron-block, alloy-head unit, but has a dry sump, bigger inlet valves, a new exhaust manifold and hotter camshafts. In its original form, with three twin-barrel Weber carburetors, it produces 250bhp – more than 30bhp more than the C-type unit. This unit was later increased to 3781cc (231ci) and with fuel injection and an improved cylinder head, it produces up to 304bhp.

Road racer

If the D-type is a little too stark for your tastes, the roadgoing version – the XKSS – is the one to choose. This later model is fitted with a proper windshield and a folding soft top. It has a road-car style interior without the central divider.

The last 16 cars were XKSS versions and were fully street legal.

Jaguar D-TYPE

Jaguar's D-type broke new ground with its semi-monocoque construction and aerodynamic design. It was perfectly at home on the fast circuit of Le Mans, where it won for three consecutive years (1955–1957).

Dry-sump lubrication

Although the D-type's XK engine is essentially identical to that used in Jaguar's roadgoing sports cars, it has a dry sump rather than a conventional wet one. The oil is kept in a separate tank and circulated by a pump, which prevents oil surge during high-speed cornering.

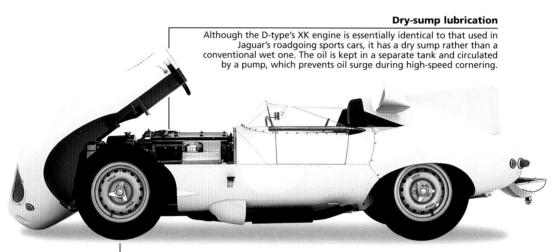

Disc brakes front and rear

Jaguar pioneered the use of disc brakes in motor racing with the C-type. The Dunlop system was also used in the D-type, being employed both front and rear.

Two-seater bodywork

Racing regulations decreed that the D-type had to be a two-seater. In reality, it raced with just a driver; a fixed cover was put over the second seat to aid aerodynamics.

Rear stabilizing fin

Part of the aerodynamic package designed by ex-Bristol Aircraft aerodynamicist Malcolm Sayer is the fin that runs back from behind the driver's headrest. This provides important directional stability when racing on very fast circuits like Le Mans.

Monocoque centre section

To give it the very stiff but light structure needed for a racing car, the D-type pioneered the use of an alloy monocoque to replace the spaceframe chassis used on the C-type. It is not a full monocoque, however, as the engine and front suspension are held in a separate subframe.

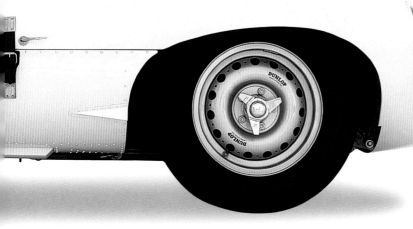

Specifications

1957 Jaguar D-type

ENGINE
Type: In-line six
Construction: Cast-iron block and alloy head
Valve gear: Two valves per cylinder operated by two overhead camshafts
Bore and stroke: 83mm (3.27in) x 106mm (4.17in)
Displacement: 3442cc (210ci)
Compression ratio: 9.0:1
Induction system: Three Weber sidedraft carburetors
Maximum power: 250bhp at 6000rpm
Maximum torque: 242lb-ft at 4000rpm
Top speed: 261km/h (162mph)
0–96km (0–60mph): 5.4 sec

TRANSMISSION
Four-speed manual

BODY/CHASSIS
Centre monocoque with separate front subframe

SPECIAL FEATURES

The spare wheel is stored in a small boot which hinges down for access.

RUNNING GEAR
Steering: Rack-and-pinion
Front suspension: Double wishbones with longitudinal torsion bars and telescopic shock absorbers
Rear suspension: Live axle with single transverse torsion bar, trailing links, single A-bracket and telescopic shock absorbers
Brakes: Dunlop discs (front and rear)
Wheels: Dunlop light alloy Centre-lock, 14cm (5.5in) x 40.6cm (16in)
Tyres: Dunlop racing, 16.5cm (6.50in) x 40.6cm (16in)

DIMENSIONS
Length: 3.9m (154.0in)
Width: 1.66m (65.4in)
Height: 1.1m (44.0in)
Wheelbase: 228cm (90.0in)
Track: 127cm (50.0in) (front), 122cm (48.0in) (rear)
Weight: 1116kg (2460lbs)

Jaguar **E-TYPE**

The E-type appeared like something from outer space in 1961. Nothing else at the price could compete with its combination of great beauty and amazing performance. It remains one of the all-time great sports cars.

"...the thrill of a lifetime."

"A combination of narrow bias-ply tyres, 265bhp and a 241km/h (150mph) top speed sounds like a real challenge, but the E-type is a joy to drive. The view down the never-ending bonnet promises the thrill of a lifetime and that's just what the E-type delivers. Power flows smoothly from the superb straight-six engine and flooring the throttle, even at 160km/h (100mph), makes the nose rise as the car surges forward toward the 241km/h (150mph) mark."

Simple but stylish – the E-type's dashboard is stocked with all the necessary gauges for a sports car.

Milestones

1961 Orders flood in

for the new Jaguar E-type, following its launch at the Geneva Motor Show.

1964 An enlarged,

4.2-litre engine is installed, giving more torque, but similar performance. An improved transmission is introduced.

The series was extended with addition of 2+2 with occasional rear seats.

1966 The larger 2+2

coupe, with small rear seats and a raised roofline is launched.

1968 Series II models have

larger bonnet opening, more prominent front and rear lights and unfaired headlights.

Series III cars have V12 engine and a more prominent grille.

1971 A new 272bhp,

5.3-litre alloy V12 is installed to form the Series III Roadster and Coupé 2+2 (the two-seater coupé is dropped). These have flared wheel arches and bolder radiator grilles. It has a top speed of more than 233km/h (145mph).

1975 Production ends

after 72,507 have been built.

UNDER THE SKIN

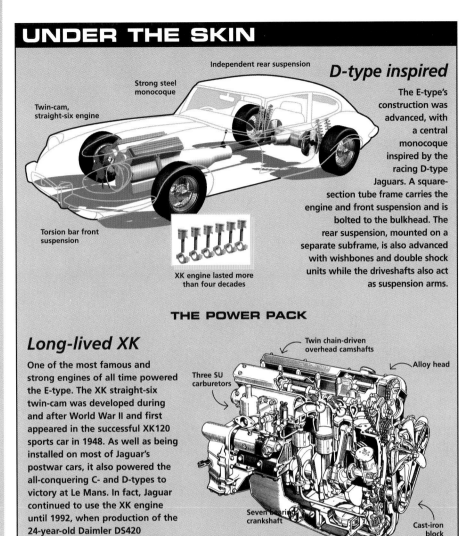

Independent rear suspension

Strong steel monocoque

Twin-cam, straight-six engine

Torsion bar front suspension

XK engine lasted more than four decades

D-type inspired

The E-type's construction was advanced, with a central monocoque inspired by the racing D-type Jaguars. A square-section tube frame carries the engine and front suspension and is bolted to the bulkhead. The rear suspension, mounted on a separate subframe, is also advanced with wishbones and double shock units while the driveshafts also act as suspension arms.

THE POWER PACK

Long-lived XK

One of the most famous and strong engines of all time powered the E-type. The XK straight-six twin-cam was developed during and after World War II and first appeared in the successful XK120 sports car in 1948. As well as being installed on most of Jaguar's postwar cars, it also powered the all-conquering C- and D-types to victory at Le Mans. In fact, Jaguar continued to use the XK engine until 1992, when production of the 24-year-old Daimler DS420 limousine finally ended.

Twin chain-driven overhead camshafts

Alloy head

Three SU carburetors

Seven bearing crankshaft

Cast-iron block

Aluminium E-type

In 1963, Jaguar built a small series of Lightweight E-types. They had aluminium monocoque and body panels rather than steel and also alloy block engines to save weight. Despite producing between 320bhp and 344bhp from their highly developed fuel-injected engines, they were outclassed on the track by Ferrari's 250 GTO.

Only 12 of the aluminium-bodied Lightweights were built.

Jaguar E-TYPE

It is no surprise the Jaguar E-type is sleek – it is the work of aerodynamicist Malcolm Sayer, with the usual input from Jaguar boss, William Lyons, himself one of the greatest English car stylists.

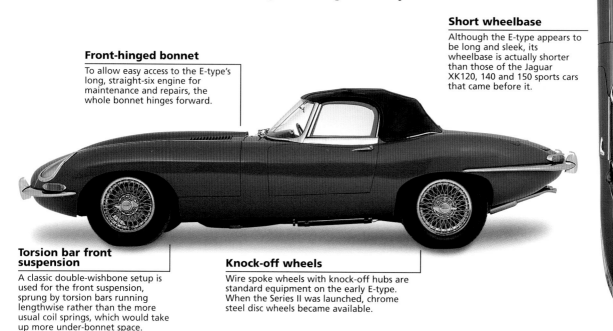

Short wheelbase

Although the E-type appears to be long and sleek, its wheelbase is actually shorter than those of the Jaguar XK120, 140 and 150 sports cars that came before it.

Front-hinged bonnet

To allow easy access to the E-type's long, straight-six engine for maintenance and repairs, the whole bonnet hinges forward.

Torsion bar front suspension

A classic double-wishbone setup is used for the front suspension, sprung by torsion bars running lengthwise rather than the more usual coil springs, which would take up more under-bonnet space.

Knock-off wheels

Wire spoke wheels with knock-off hubs are standard equipment on the early E-type. When the Series II was launched, chrome steel disc wheels became available.

Independent rear suspension

Jaguar's first car to have independent suspension was the E-type. The complete assembly is encapsulated in a separate subframe, which is attached to the monocoque via bonded rubber mountings to reduce noise transference.

Semi-monocoque construction

The E-type was built around a very strong and rigid central monocoque of sheet steel rather than on a separate chassis like some of its rivals.

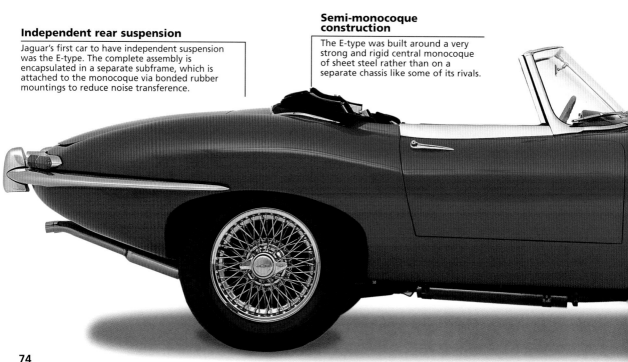

Faired-in headlights

To make the E-type even more aerodynamic, the headlights on the early cars have perspex covers, later removed due to changing Federal regulations in the US.

Inboard rear brakes

Not only does the E-type boast disc brakes all around, but they are mounted inboard at the rear, reducing unsprung weight and giving the suspension less work.

Louvred bonnet

E-types generate a lot of heat under the low bonnet, which escapes through 14 rows of louvres on the bonnet.

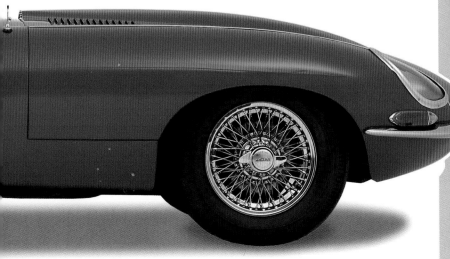

Specifications

1961 Jaguar E-Type Roadster

ENGINE

Type: Straight-six twin-cam
Construction: Cast-iron block and alloy cylinder head
Valve gear: Two valves per cylinder operated by twin chain-driven overhead camshafts
Bore and stroke: 87mm (3.43in) x 106mm (4.17in)
Displacement: 3781cc (231ci)
Compression ratio: 9.0:1
Induction system: Three SU carburetors
Maximum power: 265bhp at 5500rpm
Maximum torque: 260lb-ft at 4000rpm
Top speed: 241km/h (150mph)
0–96km (0–60mph): 7.3 sec

TRANSMISSION

Four-speed manual

BODY/CHASSIS

Steel two-seat convertible with centre steel monocoque chassis and front and rear subframes

SPECIAL FEATURES

Shallow and wide windshield needs three short wipers to keep it clear.

RUNNING GEAR

Steering: Rack-and-pinion
Front suspension: Double wishbones with longitudinal torsion bars, shocks and anti-roll bar
Rear suspension: Lower wishbones with driveshafts as upper links and twin coil spring/shock units per side
Brakes: Discs all around, inboard at rear
Wheels: Wire spoked 12.7cm (5in) x 38.1cm (15in)
Tyres: Dunlop 6.40 x 15 RS5 bias-plies

DIMENSIONS

Length: 4.45m (175.5in)
Width: 4.2m (165.3in)
Height: 1.2m (48in)
Wheelbase: 243cm (96in)
Track: 127cm (50in) (front and rear)
Weight: 1117kg (2463lbs)

Jaguar **XJ6**

In 1968, the world was amazed by the introduction of the best luxury sedan of the time. Nothing could approach its combination of ride, handling refinement, comfort and style, and certainly none came close on price.

"...beautifully engineered."

"Drive a first generation XJ6, and you'll be amazed at how modern it feels today. In 1968, it was nothing short of incredible. From the direct rack-and-pinion steering, to the smooth ride and the quiet refinement, everything feels beautifully engineered. All this is allied to handling and roadholding well beyond any contemporary sedan's. The 2.8-litre engine feels a little gutless, but the 4.2 feels swift, even today."

Inside, the XJ6 is extremely well equipped for a late-1960s British sedan.

Milestones

1964 Jaguar boss Sir William Lyons

begins to think about a replacement for the big Mk X sedan, and work on the advanced XJ6 design begins.

The Mark VII also relied on the XK straight-six engine.

1968 Launched at London's
Royal Lancaster Hotel in September, the XJ6 goes into production in 4.2-litre and 2.8-litre (180-bhp) forms with either the Jaguar four-speed and overdrive manual transmission or Borg-Warner's three-speed auto. Demand is enormous, and owners have to wait up to a year for delivery.

A much modified XJ6 with an all-new engine was launched in 1986.

1973 After over 79,000
Series I cars are made, the new Series II is launched with a raised front bumper, revised grille, and new instrument panel. A 3.4 version of the straight-six engine appears in 1975, as does a two-door coupé.

UNDER THE SKIN

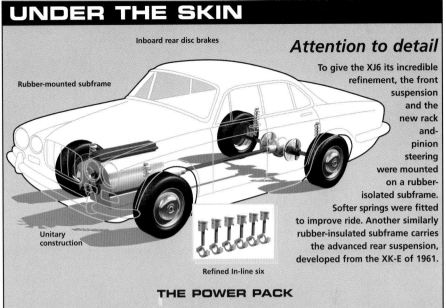

Inboard rear disc brakes

Rubber-mounted subframe

Unitary construction

Refined In-line six

Attention to detail

To give the XJ6 its incredible refinement, the front suspension and the new rack and-pinion steering were mounted on a rubber-isolated subframe. Softer springs were fitted to improve ride. Another similarly rubber-insulated subframe carries the advanced rear suspension, developed from the XK-E of 1961.

THE POWER PACK

Proven in-line six

There was never any doubt about what engine was to be used. It is Jaguar's tried-and-tested XK straight-six twin-cam designed during World War II and first seen on the XK120 in 1948. For the XJ6, it is used in 2.8- and 4.2-litre forms, offering 180 and 245bhp respectively. The iron block is topped by an alloy cylinder head, in which runs two chain-driven camshafts operating two valves per cylinder in hemispherical-shaped combustion chambers.

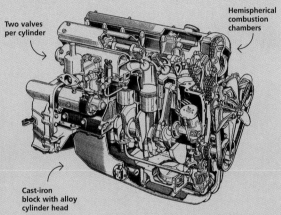

Two valves per cylinder

Hemispherical combustion chambers

Cast-iron block with alloy cylinder head

V12 monster

A V12 model followed soon after the XJ6. Powered by a huge 5.3-litre V12 engine, it offered even greater refinement and better performance. The XJ12 continued in production until 1996, and later examples are worth considering.

The XJ12s offer even greater performance and refinement.

Jaguar **XJ6**

There was nothing that could come remotely close to the XJ6 for the price. This car was so significant that current Jaguar sedans still bear similar styling cues.

Rack-and-pinion steering

Jaguar had been quick to adopt rack-and-pinion steering on its sports and racing cars, but the previous large sedan, the huge Mk X, had recirculating ball steering. This was replaced on the XJ6 by sharper and more responsive rack-and-pinion steering.

Twin-cam engine

One of the world's greatest engines powers this milestone sedan. For the XJ6 Series I, it was built in 2.8-litre and 4.2-litre forms.

Bolt-on fenders

Although the XJ6 has a modern unitary-construction monocoque, the front fenders can be unbolted for ease of repair. The monocoque is heavily reinforced with box-section cross members while more box-section chassis rails carry the rear subframe.

Inboard rear discs

The rear disc brakes are mounted inboard next to the differential for reduced unsprung weight.

Specifications

1968 Jaguar XJ6 2.8

ENGINE
Type: In-line six

Construction: Iron block and alloy head

Valve gear: Two inclined valves per cylinder operated by twin chain-driven overhead camshafts

Bore and stroke: 92mm (3.62in) x 106mm (4.17in)

Displacement: 2791cc (170ci)

Compression ratio: 9.0:1

Induction system: Two SU carburetors

Maximum power: 180bhp at 5500rpm

Maximum torque: 283lb-ft at 3750rpm

Top speed: 193km/h (120mph)

0–96km (0–60mph): 10.1 sec

TRANSMISSION
Borg-Warner three-speed auto or Jaguar four-speed plus overdrive manual

BODY/CHASSIS
Unitary construction with four-door body

SPECIAL FEATURES

A four-speed transmission with overdrive offers relaxed high-speed cruising.

The large, upright radiator grille is one of the Mk I's most distinctive features.

RUNNING GEAR
Steering: Rack-and-pinion

Front suspension: Suspension: double wishbones with coil springs, telescopic shock absorbers and anti-roll bar

Rear suspension: Wishbones, trailing arms and double coil spring/shock absorber units per side

Brakes: Discs (front and rear)

Wheels: Steel 38.1cm (15in) dia.

Tyres: Dunlop SP Sport E70VR15

DIMENSIONS
Length: 14.8m (189.5in)

Width: 1.78m (69.9in)

Height: 1.34m (52.8in)

Wheelbase: 276cm (108.8in)

Track: 147cm (58.0in) (front), 149cm (58.6in) (rear)

Weight: 1645kg (3627lbs)

Overdrive transmission
The standard XJ6 transmission is a Borg-Warner three-speed auto, but buyers could opt for Jaguar's four-speed unit with overdrive.

Jaguar **XJC**

Few people who drove Jaguar's XJ sedan were in any doubt that this was one of the world's great cars. A two-door coupé version soon followed. However, it was short-lived, bowing out after only two years.

"...excellent mid-range power."

"At idle, the V12 engine purrs magically yet will still rev enthusiastically. A very broad torque curve also gives it excellent mid-range power. As for the ride, it would be difficult to find a more comfortable car from the 1970s. A low centre of gravity and sophisticated suspension give it good roadholding and can move at a pace that will make you think you are in a smaller car. One of the few drawbacks is the wind noise from the frameless windows."

Sumptuous leather seats and a generous outlay of walnut – this could only be a Jaguar.

Milestones

1973 The new Series 2 XJ range

is launched and a coupé model is displayed. However, it will be another two years before production begins.

The original Series I XJ6 sedan made its debut in 1968, followed by a V12 version in 1972.

1975 Jaguar and Daimler badged coupé

versions of the XJ6 and XJ12 officially enter production.

Jaguar's other two-door coupé of the mid 1970s was the stylish and classic XJS.

1976 Tuning firm Broadspeed reveals

a heavily modified coupé with a 550-bhp V12, Lucas fuel injection and huge disc brakes. Two cars compete in the European Touring Car Championship.

1977 Production of the XJC comes to an end.

UNDER THE SKIN

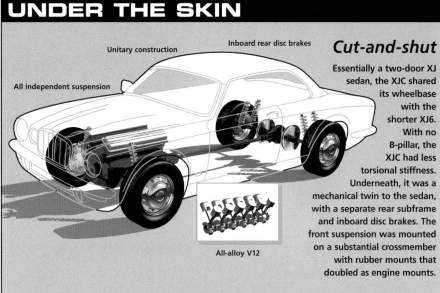

Unitary construction

Inboard rear disc brakes

All independent suspension

All-alloy V12

Cut-and-shut

Essentially a two-door XJ sedan, the XJC shared its wheelbase with the shorter XJ6. With no B-pillar, the XJC had less torsional stiffness. Underneath, it was a mechanical twin to the sedan, with a separate rear subframe and inboard disc brakes. The front suspension was mounted on a substantial crossmember with rubber mounts that doubled as engine mounts.

THE POWER PACK

Superlative V12

Although a 4.2-litre straight-six was offered on the XJC, the centre of attention was the fabulous V12 engine used in the XJ12 sedan and E-Type Series 3. All-new in 1971, this magnificent engine had a single chain-driven overhead camshaft per bank of cylinders, operating in-line valves. Carburetion came courtesy of four Stromberg CDs, although fuel injection was substituted soon after launch along with Lucas OPUS electronic ignition.

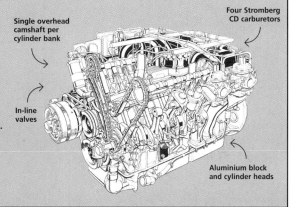

Single overhead camshaft per cylinder bank

In-line valves

Four Stromberg CD carburetors

Aluminium block and cylinder heads

12 cylinders

Of all the XJ range, the two-door coupés are the rarest and most desirable. For ultimate status and refinement, the V12 model is a must, though good ones can be expensive. A badge-engineered Daimler version, the Double-Six Coupé, was also available.

XJCs came only with 4.2- or 5.3-litre engines.

Jaguar **XJC**

Jaguar's speciality is sporty sedans and luxurious sports cars. The XJC was a unique attempt to marry the two in one enticing package. It was elegant, refined, exclusive and – with its V12 engine – a superb cruiser.

Six or twelve cylinders
The XJC used either the old XK straight-six or Jaguar's infamous 5.3-litre V12, found in the final versions of the E-Types. Compared to the six-cylinder XJC, the V12 was much more expensive and rarer – the smaller-engined versions outnumber the V12 by more than three to one.

Short wheelbase
Based on the short wheelbase XJ6 sedan, the coupé was also unique in that it was the only XJ to marry the V12 engine with the 276cm (108.8in) wheelbase chassis.

Long doors
Compared to the XJ sedan, the coupé's doors were 102mm (4in) longer and much heavier. An absence of vent windows also gave it a neater side profile.

Unique roofline
Having a unique roofline gave rise to some problems, particularly wind noise and water leaks. Neither problem was ever properly addressed by Jaguar.

Black vinyl roof

All XJ coupés had a black vinyl roof. This was less to do with aesthetics and more to do with craftiness. Chopping the front and rear roof sections of a sedan to make the coupé roofline left an unsightly seam that had to be covered up – and a vinyl roof was the cost-efficient solution.

Pillarless glass

The opportunity was taken to rid the XJ coupé of a central pillar and so do away with a glass pillar divider. Both front and rear windows could wind away out of sight to allow completely open sides.

Smaller cabin

Although the wheelbase remained the same as the sedan, rear seat room was tighter. Still, compared to most coupé competitors the XJC was very spacious.

1976 Jaguar XJ 4.2 C

ENGINE

Type: In-line six-cylinder
Construction: Cast-iron block and head
Valve gear: Two valves per cylinder operated by twin chain-driven overhead camshafts
Bore and stroke: 93mm (3.65in) x 106mm (4.17in)
Displacement: 4235cc (258ci)
Compression ratio: 7.8:1
Induction system: Two SU carburetors
Maximum power: 176bhp at 4750rpm
Maximum torque: 219lb-ft at 2500rpm
Top speed: 224km/h (139mph)
0–96km (0–60mph): 8.8 sec

TRANSMISSION

Borg Warner three-speed automatic

BODY/CHASSIS

Unitary monocoque construction chassis with two-door steel coupé body

SPECIAL FEATURES

All XJC coupés had vinyl roof coverings to hide metal seams.

RUNNING GEAR

Steering: Rack-and-pinion
Front suspension: Double wishbones with coil springs, telescopic shock absorbers and anti-roll bar
Rear suspension: Lower wishbones and radius arms with twin coil springs and telescopic shock absorbers
Brakes: Vented discs (front and rear)
Wheels: Steel or alloy 38.1cm (15in) dia.
Tyres: 205/70 VR15

DIMENSIONS

Length: 4.8m (189.5in)
Width: 1.76m (69.3in)
Height: 1.37m (54.1in)
Wheelbase: 276cm (108.8in)
Track: 147cm (58.0in) (front), 149cm (58.5in) (rear)
Weight: 1676kg (3696lbs)

Jaguar **XJR-S**

Jaguar commissioned Tom Walkinshaw to turn the luxury XJS into a real performance car. He did that brilliantly by making the engine far bigger and more powerful and improving the suspension.

"Small but expert changes."

"Just giving the XJR-S steering more weight and feel makes it seem small and agile. Stiffening the suspension complements the revised steering perfectly. The XJR-S becomes a real high-performance car that can be thrown into corners with confidence or just used as a high speed cruiser. It turns sharply, and doesn't have the same body roll through corners as the regular XJS. Its bigger tyres provide tremendous grip and give the car its fantastic roadholding ability."

There's plenty of leather and walnut in the cabin of the XJR-S. Comfort is just as important as performance in a Jaguar.

Milestones

1975 Jaguar replaces the E-type with the new XJS model.

1988 Soon after the Jaguar Sport is launched, the company builds the XJR-S. It uses the standard Jaguar 5.3-litre V12 engine, but fortifies the suspension with revised springs, shocks and bushings, along with stiffer steering.

1989 The V12 engine is given a new crankshaft with longer stroke to increase displacement to 5993cc (366ci). Power improves by 32bhp and torque by 52lb-ft.

In 1994, the standard XJS became available with the 6.0-litre engine.

1991 Jaguar slightly restyles the standard XJS, giving it a more modern look – and the XJR-S follows suit. The race-derived Zytek engine management system is improved, along with the intake manifold. A free-flowing exhaust is also added. The result is 333bhp and 365 lb-ft of torque.

1995 XJR-S production ends shortly before the new XK8 is unveiled.

UNDER THE SKIN

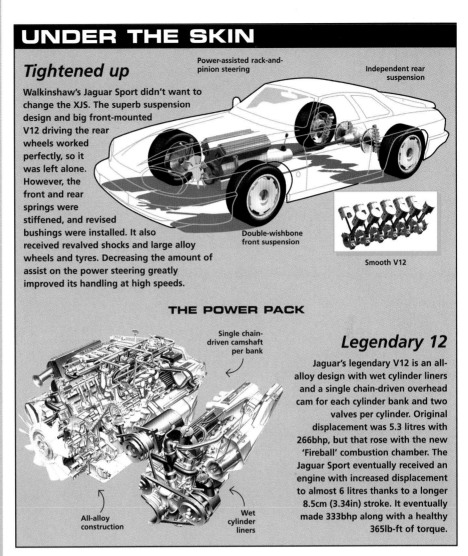

Tightened up

Walkinshaw's Jaguar Sport didn't want to change the XJS. The superb suspension design and big front-mounted V12 driving the rear wheels worked perfectly, so it was left alone. However, the front and rear springs were stiffened, and revised bushings were installed. It also received revalved shocks and large alloy wheels and tyres. Decreasing the amount of assist on the power steering greatly improved its handling at high speeds.

Power-assisted rack-and-pinion steering

Independent rear suspension

Double-wishbone front suspension

Smooth V12

THE POWER PACK

Single chain-driven camshaft per bank

All-alloy construction

Wet cylinder liners

Legendary 12

Jaguar's legendary V12 is an all-alloy design with wet cylinder liners and a single chain-driven overhead cam for each cylinder bank and two valves per cylinder. Original displacement was 5.3 litres with 266bhp, but that rose with the new 'Fireball' combustion chamber. The Jaguar Sport eventually received an engine with increased displacement to almost 6 litres thanks to a longer 8.5cm (3.34in) stroke. It eventually made 333bhp along with a healthy 365lb-ft of torque.

Best of Britain

Opinions are mixed about the looks of the XJS. Some find it bizarre, others think it's very sleek and crisp. The XJR-S, with its large-diameter alloy wheels and subtle spoilers, must rank as the best looking version of Jaguar's long-running grand tourer.

Many enthusiast were disappointed by the XKE's predecessor, the XJS.

Jaguar **XJR-S**

Needing to capitalize on its Le Mans success of 1988, Jaguar wanted a sportier high-performance car than was already in the line-up. To keep costs low, Jaguar transformed the XJS into the XJR-S instead of building a whole new model.

Three-speed auto

Only a three-speed automatic transmission was used in the XJR-S. Unfortunately, a sporty manual transmission was not available in this model.

Six-litre V12

As part of the programme to give the V12 engine more power, its displacement is increased to 6 litres by lengthening the stroke with a revised crankshaft and longer connecting rods.

Rear spoiler

A huge rear spoiler generates useful downforce to improve the XJR-S's stability at very high speeds.

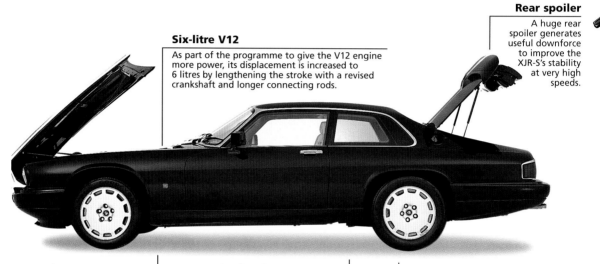

Uprated suspension

The suspension is uprated with shorter, stiffer, coil springs and Bilstein shocks complementing the bigger wheels and lower profile tyres.

Revised styling

In 1991 Jaguar restyled the XJS and the XJR-S followed suit, with softer lines to the rear windows.

Larger rear tyres

Where the XJS uses the same size tyres all around, the XJR-S has larger, 245/55 tyres on 40.6cm (16in) rather than 38.1cm (15in) wheels. The front tyres are smaller 225/50s.

Forged alloy wheels

One major difference between the XJS and XJR-S is the larger, 20.3cm (8in) x 40.6cm (16in), forged-alloy wheels fitted to the XJR-S. They are designed to provide some air flow to the brakes.

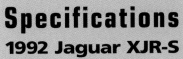

Specifications
1992 Jaguar XJR-S

ENGINE
Type: V12
Construction: Alloy block and heads, wet cylinder liners
Valve gear: Two valves per cylinder operated by single chain-driven camshaft per bank of cylinders
Bore and stroke: 90mm (3.54in) x 78mm (3.07in)
Displacement: 5993cc (366ci)
Compression ratio: 11.0:1
Induction system: Zytek sequential electronic fuel injection
Maximum power: 333bhp at 5250rpm
Maximum torque: 365lb-ft at 3650rpm
Top Speed: 249km/h (155mph)
0–96km/h (0–60mph): 4.8 seconds

TRANSMISSION
Three-speed automatic

BODY/CHASSIS
Steel monocoque with two-door coupé body

SPECIAL FEATURES

Rear seats are luxurious but leg room is a little bit limited.

RUNNING GEAR
Steering: Rack-and-pinion
Front suspension: Double wishbones with coil springs, Bilstein telescopic shocks and anti-roll bar
Rear suspension: Lower wishbone with upper link and radius arms, coil springs and Bilstein telescopic shocks
Brakes: Vented discs, 28.4cm (11.2in) dia. (front), 10.3in dia. (rear)
Wheels: Forged alloy, 8in x 16in
Tyres: Dunlop D40 M2, 225/50 ZR16 (front), 245/55 ZR16 (rear)

DIMENSIONS
Length: 4.82m (189.8in)
Width: 1.79m (70.6in)
Height: 1.25m (49.2in)
Wheelbase: 259cm (102in)
Track: 149cm (58.6in) (front), 150cm (59.2in) (rear)
Weight: 1825kg (4023lbs)

Integrated bumper and spoiler
To improve aerodynamic efficiency and stability, the XJR-S has a chin spoiler integrated into the body-coloured front bumper.

Restyled taillights
Another feature of the 1991 restyle was the move from separate tail lights that joined the top of the rear wing to these wide rectangular lights.

Recalibrated power steering
Traditionally Jaguars have always had strong power assistance, which made the steering extremely light. The XJR-S was recalibrated for a more direct, heavier feel.

Jaguar **XJ220**

Hand-made by craftsmen and race-proven at Le Mans, the XJ220 was the sporting Jaguar for the 21st century. Yet the prototype of this superb machine was built without funding, and on their own time, by Jaguar's engineers.

"...a predator ready to pounce."

"Sit in most supercars, and you will find that creature comforts definitely take second place to performance. But the XJ220 is unique, cocooning you in traditional Jaguar luxury. The interior reeks of sumptuous leather. Air conditioning? Of course! Settle back – there's room for the tallest driver. But make no mistake, this cat crouches low like a predator ready to pounce: 160km/h (100mph) is reached in just 7.3 seconds when you floor the accelerator. The mid-rear engine placement assures beautiful balance, and the chassis offers massive structural integrity."

The wrap-around dash houses a complete set of instruments. Despite the car's performance, this is no stripped-down racing car, but a luxury Jaguar.

Milestones

1988 The XJ220 prototype is unveiled to cheers at the British International Auto Show. Designed in secret, it has a 12-cylinder 5999cc (366ci) motor, all-wheel drive and a planned top speed of 322km/h (200mph) plus. Dozens of potential buyers come forward: "We'll have one – at any price."

The XJ220 made full use of Jaguar's endurance racing technology.

1989 Jaguar announces "the XJ220 you can buy" with a 24-valve V6 turbocharged engine, rear-wheel drive – and a planned top speed of more than 354km/h (220mph); 350 orders are accepted from 1000 applications.

1992 In testing at Nardo, Italy an XJ220 achieves 349.7km/h (217.3mph), making it the world's fastest production road car – a tag now assumed by the smaller McLaren F1. Given a long enough straightaway, it should be possible for the XJ220 to reach the magic 354km/h (220mph).

1994 The last of the 281 production run of XJ220s come off the line. A price of $706,000 made it impossible to sell every car in a world hit by recession, but those who did take delivery, like rock star Elton John, own the fastest Jaguar ever.

UNDER THE SKIN

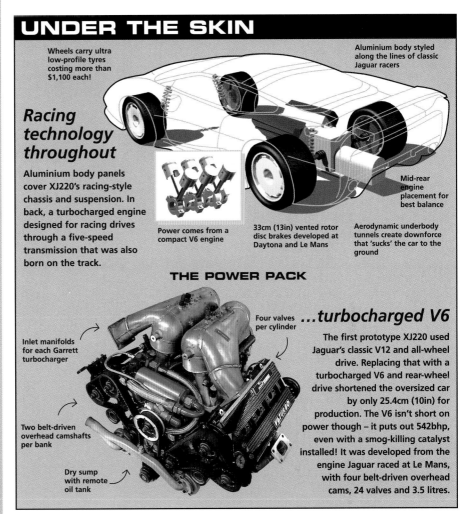

Wheels carry ultra low-profile tyres costing more than $1,100 each!

Aluminium body styled along the lines of classic Jaguar racers

Racing technology throughout

Aluminium body panels cover XJ220's racing-style chassis and suspension. In back, a turbocharged engine designed for racing drives through a five-speed transmission that was also born on the track.

Power comes from a compact V6 engine

Mid-rear engine placement for best balance

33cm (13in) vented rotor disc brakes developed at Daytona and Le Mans

Aerodynamic underbody tunnels create downforce that 'sucks' the car to the ground

THE POWER PACK

Inlet manifolds for each Garrett turbocharger

Two belt-driven overhead camshafts per bank

Dry sump with remote oil tank

Four valves per cylinder

...turbocharged V6

The first prototype XJ220 used Jaguar's classic V12 and all-wheel drive. Replacing that with a turbocharged V6 and rear-wheel drive shortened the oversized car by only 25.4cm (10in) for production. The V6 isn't short on power though – it puts out 542bhp, even with a smog-killing catalyst installed! It was developed from the engine Jaguar raced at Le Mans, with four belt-driven overhead cams, 24 valves and 3.5 litres.

Elegant strength

Although constructed mostly from aluminium, the XJ220 is no lightweight. Its smooth, sensuous lines hide an extremely advanced honeycomb construction. The immensely strong panels and chassis give the car massive structural integrity – after its government crash test, the XJ220's glazing remained intact, and all doors and rear panels opened normally!

Open lids of radiator, engine and tiny luggage compartment.

Jaguar **XJ220** 🇬🇧

Elegant and smooth, the XJ220 took its styling cues from the XJ13, a still-born Jaguar racer of the 1960s. But under the skin it's right up to date, with state-of-the-art racing technology.

Baggage space

This is a car for travelling light. The rear end is full of engine, and the front is full of radiators to cool it. The boot is just big enough for a briefcase or two.

Transparent engine cover

The hood on the XJ220 is a lift-up glass panel that puts the powerful turbo motor permanently on show.

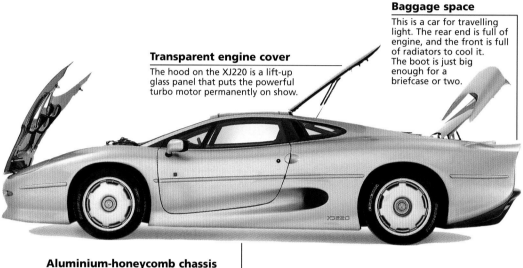

Aluminium-honeycomb chassis

Designed to be simple and easy to produce (because the first XJ220 was built in the Jaguar engineers' spare time), the chassis is bonded together with adhesive, not welded.

V6 turbo engine

Light and compact, the engine was designed for Jaguar's IMSA race cars in the late-1980s. Adapted for road use, it produces 542bhp, more than the big V12 originally planned for the car.

Luxury interior

Leather seats, lush carpets and a top-level sound system ensure that XJ220 owners know they're in a Jaguar.

Aluminium body

Lightweight aluminium is used for the body. Each car was hand-assembled before being painted one of five standard colours – all metallics. Cars were available in silver, grey, blue, green and maroon.

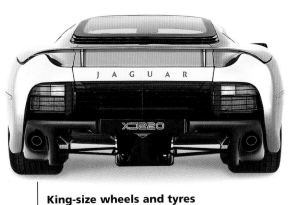

King-size wheels and tyres

Specially designed tyres and wheels are so big there's no room for a spare. If a tyre goes flat, it's filled with a special aerosol mixture and can be driven up to 96km (60 miles) at 48km/h (30mph).

Aerodynamic styling

Designed to look as elegant as a Jaguar should, the XJ220 is also aerodynamically efficient. At high speeds, the car develops over nearly 272kg (600lbs) of downforce to hold it on the road.

Street legal

The XJ220 is legal for road use in most parts of the world, but not in the US. Jaguar never exported any cars to the States, although 10 were sent there for a TV race series in 1993.

Specifications
1993 Jaguar XJ220

ENGINE

Type: V6 turbocharged, 60°
Construction: Aluminium alloy block and heads
Bore and stroke: 94mm (3.7in) x 84mm (3.3in)
Displacement: 3494cc (213ci)
Compression ratio: 8.3:1
Induction system: Electronic injection with twin Garrett turbochargers with air-to-air intercoolers and wastegate control
Maximum power: 542bhp at 7200rpm
Maximum torque: 475lb-ft at 4500rpm
Top Speed: 335km/h (208mph)
0–96km/h (0–60mph): 3.8 sec

TRANSMISSION

Transaxle: FF Developments all-synchromesh, five-speed manual transaxle with triple-cone synchronizer on first and second gears; Viscous control limited-slip differential

BODY/CHASSIS

Aluminium alloy honeycomb monocoque with alloy two-door, two-seat body

SPECIAL FEATURES

Vents behind doors feed air to engine's twin intercoolers.

RUNNING GEAR

Front suspension: Independent, double unequal-length wishbones, push-rod and rocker-operated spring/shock units, anti-roll bar
Rear suspension: Independent, unequal-length double wishbones, rocker-operated twin spring/shock units, anti-roll bar
Brakes: Vented 33cm (13in) (front), 30cm (11.8in) (rear), four-piston calipers
Wheels: Die-cast aluminium alloy. 22.8cm (9in) x 43.2cm (17in) (front), 25.4cm (10in) x 45.7cm (18in) (rear)
Tyres: 255/45 ZR17 (front), 345/35 ZR18 (rear)

DIMENSIONS

Length: 4.93m (194in)
Width: 2.2m (87.4in)
Height: 1.15m (45.3in)
Wheelbase: 264cm (103.9in)
Track: 171cm (67.3in) (front), 159cm (62.5in) (rear)
Weight: 1470kg (3241lbs)

Jenson INTERCEPTOR

Unveiled in 1966, the Interceptor had everything: Italian styling, American V8 power and well-balanced handling. The original Interceptor remained in production, virtually unaltered, for 10 years and gained a cult following that lives on today.

"...a sense of refinement."

"More of a grand tourer than a sports car, the Interceptor has deep, comfortable seats. The powerful American V8 and automatic transmission are perfectly suited to a laid-back approach to driving and give the car a sense of refinement. Despite its mannerisms, the car is quick and can reach 96km/h (60mph) in just over six seconds. Despite its weight, the Jensen has predictable handling, but the brakes are hard-pressed to stop it at speeds above 200km/h (124mph)."

Full instrumentation is standard and the interior trim is of the highest quality.

Milestones

1966 Jensen
presents two vehicles styled by Vingale at the London Motor Show. One is fitted with a specially developed four-wheel drive system.

Jensen's 1954 541 had triple carburetors and four-wheel disc brakes

1969 An improved
Mk II Interceptor is launched. It has a bigger fuel tank, radial tyres and restyled bumpers.

1971 The Mk III and
an SP model with three two-barrel carburetors and 330bhp are introduced. The FF is dropped this year.

1976 Jensen goes
out of business and the last original Interceptor is built.

The forerunner of the Interceptor was the bizarre-looking CV8.

1983 A new Mk IV
Interceptor enters production, built by Jensen Parts and Service.

UNDER THE SKIN

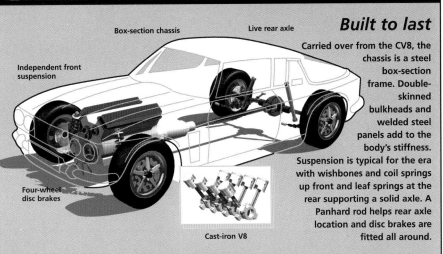

Box-section chassis

Live rear axle

Independent front suspension

Four-wheel disc brakes

Cast-iron V8

Built to last

Carried over from the CV8, the chassis is a steel box-section frame. Double-skinned bulkheads and welded steel panels add to the body's stiffness. Suspension is typical for the era with wishbones and coil springs up front and leaf springs at the rear supporting a solid axle. A Panhard rod helps rear axle location and disc brakes are fitted all around.

THE POWER PACK

Chrysler V8 power

Original Interceptors are powered by Chrysler 6.3-litre (383ci) and 7.2-litre (440ci) V8s. Both engines are made of cast-iron with chain-driven camshafts, a five main-bearing crankshaft and two valves per cylinder. With the larger unit, acceleration is phenomenal, although handling naturally suffers. Mark IV cars use a small-block 5.9-litre V8, based on the early 340ci unit. This produced improved fuel economy and slightly better handling.

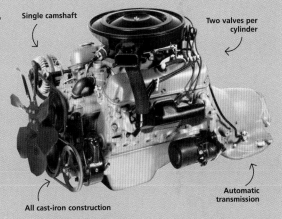

Single camshaft

Two valves per cylinder

All cast-iron construction

Automatic transmission

Hi-tech FF

Standing for Ferguson Formula, the Jensen FF has four-wheel drive, rack-and-pinion steering and anti-lock brakes. Slightly longer than the standard Interceptor, it is a complex machine and only 320 were built. Only a small number still remain today.

The Jensen FF was in production from 1966 to 1971.

Jenson **INTERCEPTOR**

The Jensen Interceptor, launched in 1966 at the London Motor Show, is by far the company's best-remembered product and its biggest seller. The car was so good that it was reborn in the early 1980s.

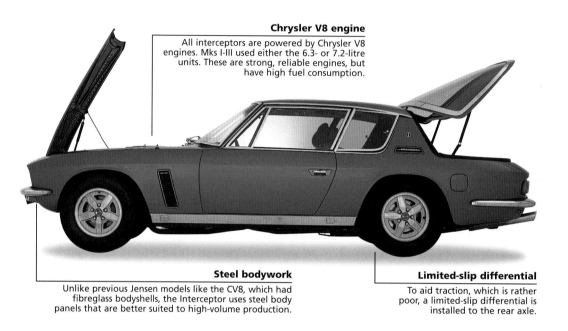

Chrysler V8 engine

All interceptors are powered by Chrysler V8 engines. Mks I-III used either the 6.3- or 7.2-litre units. These are strong, reliable engines, but have high fuel consumption.

Steel bodywork

Unlike previous Jensen models like the CV8, which had fibreglass bodyshells, the Interceptor uses steel body panels that are better suited to high-volume production.

Limited-slip differential

To aid traction, which is rather poor, a limited-slip differential is installed to the rear axle.

Glass hatchback

The bulbous back window is not only attractive, but also functional. The whole unit lifts up to provide space for luggage.

Specifications

1968 Jensen Interceptor

ENGINE
Type: V8

Construction: Cast-iron block and heads

Valve gear: Two valves per cylinder operated by hydraulic tappets, pushrods and rockers

Bore and stroke: 108mm (4.25in) x 86mm (3.38in)

Displacement: 6276cc (383ci)

Compression ratio: 10.0:1

Induction system: Single Carter AFB four-barrel carburetor

Maximum power: 330bhp at 4600rpm

Maximum torque: 450lb-ft at 2800rpm

Top Speed: 209km/h (130mph)

0–96km/h (0–60mph): 8 seconds

TRANSMISSION
Chrysler TorqueFlite 727 automatic

BODY/CHASSIS
Tubular and welded sheet steel monocoque with two-door body

SPECIAL FEATURES

Fender extractor vents aid engine cooling and help to distinguish the Interceptor from the four-wheel drive FF, which has two vents per side.

RUNNING GEAR
Steering: Recirculating ball

Front suspension: Independent wishbones with coil springs and telescopic shocks

Rear suspension: Live rear axle with semi-elliptical leaf springs, telescopic shocks and a Panhard rod

Brakes: Girling discs, 29cm (11.4in) dia. (front), 27.2cm (10.7in) dia. (rear)

Wheels: Rostyle pressed steel, 38.1cm (15in) dia.

Tyres: Dunlop 185 x 15

DIMENSIONS
Length: 4.78m (188in)

Width: 1.78m (70in)

Height: 1.35m (53in)

Wheelbase: 267cm (105in)

Track: 142cm (56in) (front and rear)

Weight: 1676kg (3696lbs)

Adjustable shocks

Despite its archaic rear leaf springs, the Interceptor has adjustable telescopic shocks to help smooth out the ride.

Italian styling

The shape was originally penned by Touring of Milan and adapted by Vignale to produce the Interceptor.

Land Rover **DEFENDER**

First seen in 1948, the classic Land Rover shape continues today as the Defender. Rugged, durable and able to travel further than almost any off-roader, it has become a legend among both four-wheel drive enthusiasts and the world's armed forces.

"...Unstoppable in any terrain."

"With its torquey V8 engine, the Defender has the ability to get out of any sticky situation. In the rugged outdoors, the Defender is unstoppable in any terrain. Thanks to its 10 forward gears, lockable differential, superb ground clearance, minimal overhangs and four-wheel drive, the Defender can climb a 45° slope and wade through rivers more than 51cm (20in) deep. The light, damped steering, well-judged springing and extremely long-travel suspension make light work of deep ruts."

The Defender's interior is very basic, with hard-wearing trim material and a rubber floormat.

Milestones

1948 The first Land Rover is launched with a 203cm (80in) wheelbase, and it is modelled on the Willys Jeep.

1958 In the Series II the four-cylinder engine increases from 2.0 litres to 2.3 litres.

Series I Land Rovers were extremely basic in specification.

1971 The Series III is fitted with full synchromesh, a new grille and a safety instrument panel.

1979 The V8 engine becomes an option.

The British Army uses many special versions of the Land Rover.

1985 Restyled Ninety and One-Ten models are built with 229cm (90in) and 279cm (110in) wheelbases.

1990 Revised Defender range is launched, taking the rugged Land Rover towards the end of the millennium.

UNDER THE SKIN

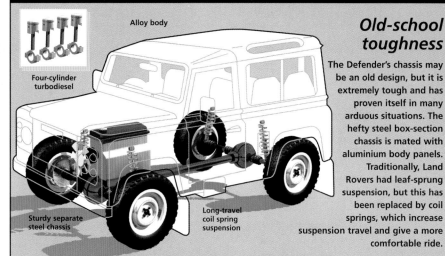

Four-cylinder turbodiesel

Alloy body

Sturdy separate steel chassis

Long-travel coil spring suspension

Old-school toughness

The Defender's chassis may be an old design, but it is extremely tough and has proven itself in many arduous situations. The hefty steel box-section chassis is mated with aluminium body panels. Traditionally, Land Rovers had leaf-sprung suspension, but this has been replaced by coil springs, which increase suspension travel and give a more comfortable ride.

THE POWER PACK

V8 or turbodiesel

There is a choice of engines for the Defender. Rover's venerable all-alloy, ex-Buick V8 has given sterling service in the Land Rover. The engine is lightweight, compact and could produce 182bhp, but it is tuned for maximum torque rather than outright power. For many customers the four-cylinder, 113bhp 2.5-litre turbodiesel engine is the preferred choice because it is economical and has immense torque.

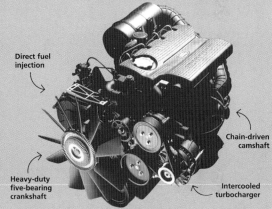

Direct fuel injection

Chain-driven camshaft

Heavy-duty five-bearing crankshaft

Intercooled turbocharger

Short and sweet

The Defender is built in two wheelbase lengths – 229cm (90in) and 279cm (110in). The shorter version, powered by a V8 engine, is the better model, as it is lighter and has improved off-road performance. Even in this short version, the station wagon body can seat up to seven people comfortably.

The 229cm (90in) Defender 90 powered with a V8 is one tough off-road vehicle.

Land Rover **DEFENDER**

This is the quintessential, go-anywhere, no-nonsense off-roader. It may appear utilitarian when compared with the more recent sports-utility competition, but for pure ability the Defender is hard to beat.

Overhang

Minimal front and rear body overhang are essential for climbing ability. The Defender is capable of an approach angle of 48°, along with a departure angle of 45°.

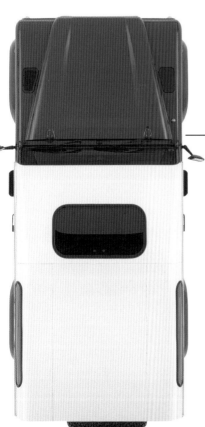

Aluminium body

For light weight, the very stiff bodywork is made of aluminium. All of the panels can be easily replaced if they become damaged. The aluminium body is also more resistant to corrosion than steel.

Ground clearance

With 21cm (8.3in) of ground clearance, the Defender can clear most obstacles in its path. All major components are well protected and electrical equipment is waterproofed, allowing the Defender to splash through rivers up to 51cm (20in) deep.

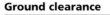

Seating for seven

Up to seven people can be carried in the Defender 90 – three up front and four in the back. The longer wheelbase Defender 110 model can seat nine.

Coil-sprung axles

Live axles front and rear are both rugged and adaptable. For many years, the Land Rover suffered from its very stiff leaf springs, but now it has coil springs and telescopic shocks all around.

Turbodiesel power

The older V8 gives better performance but has much higher fuel consumption than the four-cylinder turbodiesel engine. In addition, the turbodiesel achieves maximum torque at a very low 1800rpm.

Specifications
1997 Land Rover Defender 90 TDi

ENGINE

Type: In-line four-cylinder turbodiesel
Construction: Iron cylinder block and alloy head
Valve gear: Two valves per cylinder operated by a single overhead camshaft
Bore and stroke: 90mm (3.56in) x 97mm (3.81in)
Displacement: 2500cc (153ci)
Compression ratio: 19.5:1
Induction system: Direct fuel injection with intercooler and turbocharger
Maximum power: 113bhp at 4000rpm
Maximum torque: 194lb-ft at 1800rpm
Top Speed: 140kmh (87mph)
0–96km/h (0–60mph): not known

TRANSMISSION

Five-speed manual with transfer case

BODY/CHASSIS

Aluminium three-door body on steel chassis

SPECIAL FEATURES

Flip-down steps allow easy access to the extremely high driver's cab.

RUNNING GEAR

Steering: Worm-and-roller
Front suspension: Live axle with coil springs and shocks
Rear suspension: Live axle with coil springs and shocks
Brakes: Discs (front and rear)
Wheels: Steel, 40.6cm (16in) dia.
Tyres: BF Goodrich All-Terrain 205/R16

DIMENSIONS

Length: 3.99m (157.1in)
Width: 1.79m (70.5in)
Height: 2.03m (80.2in)
Wheelbase: 236cm (92.9in)
Track: 149cm (58.5in) (front), 149cm (58.5in) (rear)
Weight: 1695kg (3737lbs)

Land Rover **FREELANDER**

This British firm has always produced tough, go-anywhere off-roaders – real all-terrain machines. The Freelander is Land Rover's first move into a crossover market where fun road cars and off-roaders join up. It is smaller than other Land Rovers but has proved just as popular.

"...extremely accomplished."

"The Freelander's natural habitat is suburban streets, and in this role it is extremely accomplished. The performance is perfectly adequate, if not exciting, while the handling is hardly distinguishable from a very good road car – you just roll more because of the higher centre of gravity. Off road, the Freelander struggles to climb steep slopes since there is no low-speed transfer case, but in most respects it copes admirably."

The Freelander is more traditional inside than some of its rivals.

Milestones

1997 The Freelander makes its international debut at the September Frankfurt Motor Show.

1997 In October, the car appears at the British Motor Show at Earl's Court, London.

Land Rovers have been in production since 1948 and are used around the world.

1998 The Freelander first goes on sale with 1.8-litre gasoline and 2.0-litre diesel engines and as a two- or four-door model. Unlike the larger Discovery, the Freelander is not offered on the US market.

Bigger brother to the Freelander is the high-roof Discovery.

1999 Having proved a commercial success, the Freelander continues into the new model year with few changes.

UNDER THE SKIN

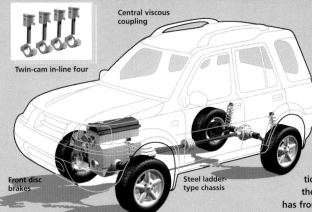

Central viscous coupling

Twin-cam in-line four

Front disc brakes

Steel ladder-type chassis

Monocoque

The Freelander marks a departure from other Land Rovers in adopting unitary construction, with a steel ladder-type chassis bonded to the body. Coil-sprung live axles are fitted front and rear, with a central viscous coupling and electronic traction control in place of a conventional differential. Like most of the competition, the Freelander has front disc and rear drum brakes.

THE POWER PACK

MGF powerplant

The standard Freelander engine is a version of the acclaimed 1.8-litre K-series four-cylinder unit, tuned for low-down torque (the maximum of 122lb-ft comes at just 2750rpm). It is of all-aluminium construction, with a twin-cam cylinder head and sequential multipoint fuel injection. The engine is mounted up front across the engine bay – a first for Land Rover. Although it produces just 119bhp, the K-series impresses by its smoothness, refinement, willingness and rev-happy nature.

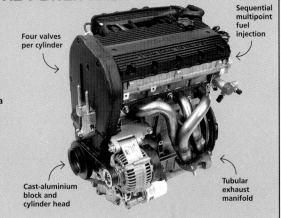

Four valves per cylinder

Sequential multipoint fuel injection

Cast-aluminium block and cylinder head

Tubular exhaust manifold

Stylish softback

Many prefer the 1.8-litre gas engine, but the diesel model is the one to chose if you want torque and fuel economy. The other choice concerns body style, which is up to personal preference. The five-door station wagon is conventionally styled, but the more striking three-door softback has a rear that can operate as an open pickup or as a regular station wagon.

The softback model is the most desirable for young people.

Land Rover **FREELANDER**

The Freelander marks a new generation for Land Rover as a compact sport-utility vehicle. It is enjoyable and capable on the motorways as well as off-roading, and with looks that endear it to fashion-conscious buyers.

Side-opening tailgate

The huge rear door opens to the side for easy access. Extra interior space is freed up by mounting the spare wheel on the tailgate. The power rear window drops downwards.

Conventional transmission

Unlike other Land Rovers, which have two-speed transfer boxes, the Freelander relies on a normal five-speed transmission. To compensate slightly for the lack of low-speed transfer ratios, it has a low 3.25:1 first gear ratio and a very low axle ratio of 4.20:1.

Unitary construction

Unlike any other Land Rover, the Freelander has an integral body/chassis construction. The substantial steel ladder-type chassis is just grafted onto the body. This saves weight yet keeps the structure very strong and rigid for long-term fit and durability.

Electronic traction control

The ETC system uses the anti-lock braking mechanism to apply braking force to a wheel that is losing traction. At the same time, torque is fed to the wheel on the opposite side to give traction in slippery conditions.

'Intelligent' four-wheel drive

Off-roaders must have permanent four-wheel drive, but the Freelander does without a centre differential to join the front and rear drives. Instead it incorporates a central viscous coupling that, combined with electronic traction control, leads Land Rover to claim that this is an intelligent all-wheel drive system.

Trendy styling

To appeal to a younger generation of buyers, the Freelander was styled by Gerry McGovern of MGF fame. The shape attempts to mate an image of solidity with sporty elements such as the steep A-pillars and rounded fenders.

Specifications

1998 Land Rover Freelander 1.8i

ENGINE
Type: In-line four-cylinder
Construction: Aluminium block and head
Valve gear: Four valves per cylinder operated by twin overhead camshafts
Bore and stroke: 80mm (3.15in) x 89mm (3.51in)
Displacement: 1796cc (110ci)
Compression ratio: 9.5:1
Induction system: Sequential multipoint fuel injection
Maximum power: 119bhp at 5550rpm
Maximum torque: 122lb-ft at 2750rpm
Top Speed: 174km/h (108mph)
0–96km (0–60mph): 10.5 sec

TRANSMISSION
Five-speed manual

BODY/CHASSIS
A monocoque configuration with a steel five-door station wagon style body

SPECIAL FEATURES

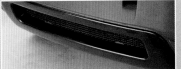

The bumper-mounted grille contains a filter to prevent ingestion of dirt.

The spare wheel mounting also incorporates the third brake light.

RUNNING GEAR
Steering: Rack-and-pinion
Front suspension: MacPherson struts with lower arms, coil springs and telescopic shock absorbers
Rear suspension: MacPherson struts with trapezoidal link, coil springs and telescopic shock absorbers
Brakes: Discs (front), drums (rear)
Wheels: Steel, 38.1cm (15in) dia.
Tyres: 195/80 HR15

DIMENSIONS
Length: 4.37m (172.2in)
Width: 2.07m (81.6in)
Height: 1.76m (69.2in)
Wheelbase: 256cm (100.6in)
Track: 153cm (60.4in) (front); 154cm (60.8in) (rear)
Weight: 1401kg (3088lbs)

Lotus OMEGA

Designed to be the ultimate flagship for GM subsidiaries Vauxhall and Opel, this high-performance super sedan was easily the fastest production four-door in the world. With its twin-turbo straight-six engine, it can out-accelerate a Ferrari Testarossa and has a staggering top speed.

"...huge grip and poise."

"Don't judge the Lotus Omega by its looks; just imagine it has the body of a Lamborghini. Yes, it's that fast. In 11 seconds, it's hitting 160km/h (100mph). In 24 seconds, you're doing 225km/h (140mph) and it's still pulling hard. Even at these speeds, it remains rock stable and rides well. And braking is just as incredible. The Omega's sheer size might feel a little clumsy on small roads, but on fast, open roads nothing can touch its combination of huge grip and poise."

A six-speed shifter and close-fitting bucket seats are the only notable changes inside.

Milestones

1988 GM starts
Lotus on the project that will become the Vauxhall Lotus Carlton (and the almost identical Opel Lotus Omega). The car is unveiled at the Geneva Motor Show the following March.

Back in the 1960s, Lotus converted the 'cooking' Cortina Mk 1 into a legendary sports sedan.

1990 Production
begins with Carltons and Omegas transported to the Lotus factory in Hethel, where Lotus technicians install a twin-turbo straight-six engine and six-speed transmission, and modify the chassis, suspension and exterior.

Lotus used the Vauxhall Carlton/Opel Omega GSi 3000 as the basis for its 274km/h (170mph) supercar.

1992 Production
ends after 950 cars have been built. GM had planned to produce 1100, but the onset of a major recession results in a fall in demand.

UNDER THE SKIN

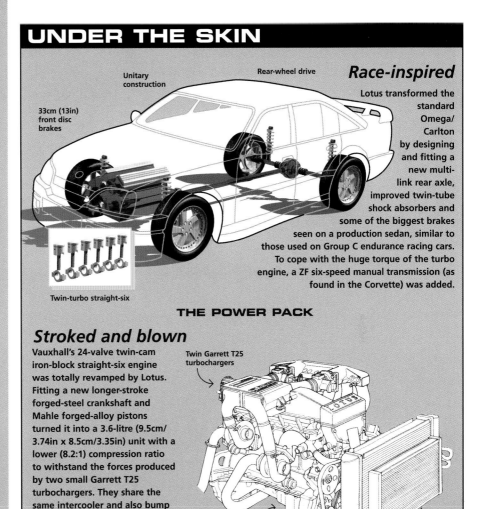

Unitary construction

Rear-wheel drive

33cm (13in) front disc brakes

Twin-turbo straight-six

Race-inspired

Lotus transformed the standard Omega/ Carlton by designing and fitting a new multi-link rear axle, improved twin-tube shock absorbers and some of the biggest brakes seen on a production sedan, similar to those used on Group C endurance racing cars. To cope with the huge torque of the turbo engine, a ZF six-speed manual transmission (as found in the Corvette) was added.

THE POWER PACK

Stroked and blown

Vauxhall's 24-valve twin-cam iron-block straight-six engine was totally revamped by Lotus. Fitting a new longer-stroke forged-steel crankshaft and Mahle forged-alloy pistons turned it into a 3.6-litre (9.5cm/ 3.74in x 8.5cm/3.35in) unit with a lower (8.2:1) compression ratio to withstand the forces produced by two small Garrett T25 turbochargers. They share the same intercooler and also bump power up to 377bhp, ensuring masses of torque to move the relatively heavy Omega.

Twin Garrett T25 turbochargers

Cast-iron block and alloy head

Air-to-air intercooler

Ferrari killer

One of the best GM cars in recent years is the Lotus Omega. It offers unbelievable performance yet has five seats and a sizable boot. A total of 510 left-hand drive Lotus Omegas were built, the rest being right-hand drive Carltons.

All cars were assembled in the UK, although most were Lotus Omegas.

Lotus OMEGA

The look of the Lotus Omega/Carlton suggests high performance, but this is a genuine 377bhp twin-turbo monster that is capable of seating five people in the utmost comfort.

Twin turbos
Although the straight-six could have been fed by a single turbocharger, Lotus opted for two smaller Garrett T25 units because the smaller rotors spin faster and hence the boost comes quicker.

Lotus suspension
Although the front MacPherson strut suspension is nearly stock except for its different camber settings, the rear has extra locating links and progressive rate springs fitted.

Larger wheels
Huge 43.2cm (17in) diameter, forged-alloy five-spoke Ronal wheels are standard on the Lotus Omega. The front ones are 21.6cm (8.5in) across and those at the rear are 24.1cm (9.5in).

Leather interior
The interior has leather upholstery and more supportive front and rear seats.

Rear spoiler
At 274km/h (170mph), downforce is of utmost importance, and huge rear spoilers are often fitted to cars capable of such speeds. The Lotus Omega, however, is an exception to this rule.

Rocker extensions

To help stability at speeds above 274km/h (170mph), the Omega has special Lotus-developed rocker panel extensions to prevent excess air from getting underneath the car and causing unwanted lift.

Huge tyres

The larger wheels carry ultra-low-profile 235/45 and 265/40 ZR17 tyres.

Specifications

1990 Lotus Omega

ENGINE

Type: In-line six

Construction: Cast-iron block and alloy cylinder head

Valve gear: Four valves per cylinder operated by twin overhead camshafts

Bore and stroke: 95mm (3.74in) x 85mm (3.35in)

Displacement: 3615cc (221ci)

Compression ratio: 8.2:1

Induction system: Electronic fuel injection with two Garrett T25 turbochargers and a single intercooler

Maximum power: 377bhp at 5200rpm

Maximum torque: 419lb-ft at 4200rpm

Top Speed: 283km/h (176mph)

0–96km (0–60mph): 5.1 sec

TRANSMISSION

ZF six-speed manual

BODY/CHASSIS

Unitary construction with four-door body

SPECIAL FEATURES

The word Lotus stamped on the cam cover indicates something special.

RUNNING GEAR

Steering: Recirculating ball

Front suspension: MacPherson struts with anti-roll bar

Rear suspension: Multi-link with progressive rate coil springs and telescopic shock absorbers

Brakes: Vented discs, 33cm (13in) dia. (front), solid discs, 30cm (11.8in) dia. (rear)

Wheels: Ronal forged-alloy, 21.6cm (8.5in) x 43.2cm (17in) (front), 24.1cm (9.5in) x 43.2cm (17in) (rear)

Tyres: 235/45 ZR17 (front), 265/40 ZR17 (rear)

DIMENSIONS

Length: 4.78m (187.7in)

Width: 1.93m (76.1in)

Height: 1.44m (56.5in)

Wheelbase: 273cm (107.5in)

Track: 144.5cm (56.9in) (front), 147cm (57.8in) (rear)

Weight: 1651kg (3640lbs)

Lotus ELISE

Generally recognized as one of the best chassis in the world, the Elise was criticized for not having enough power. Lotus has rectified this by acquiring the VVC engine from MG and creating the 143bhp Elise 111S.

"...instant power."

"The Elise cockpit has no frills. You sit close to the ground, adding to the feeling that you are driving a go-kart. As the car is so light, acceleration is fantastic, but it is when overtaking that you notice the difference between a 111S and the base Elise. The power delivery is instant, the gear change is slick and the revs just keep rising. The grip levels are so high that you are more likely to reach your own limits than the Elise's."

Exposed aluminium is used to create a clinical yet sporting interior.

Milestones

1966 Lotus launches its first
mid-engined sports car, the Europa. It uses a modified Renault 16 engine and shares some chassis components with the Elan. Lambasted for its lack of power, it was nevertheless regarded as the best-handling car in the world at the time.

The Elise was a make-or-break car for Lotus when it was launched.

1995 With a range consisting
solely of the aging Esprit, Lotus displays its new concept for a small, simple sports car: the Elise.

With its agile chassis, the Elise is well-suited to sports-car racing.

1996 The Elise is launched
to universal praise, especially for its chassis, although its looks are not to everybody's taste. Critics unite over a call for more power.

1999 Lotus rectifies the power
shortage by installing the 143bhp 1.8-litre engine from the MGF. The new model is called the 111S.

UNDER THE SKIN

Highly regarded

The Elise chassis is practically unchanged from the basic car to the 111S. This means that the midmounted engine layout and double-wishbone suspension with coil springs remain. To save weight, the spaceframe chassis is epoxy bonded. Anti-roll bars are fitted front and rear, as are vented disc brakes. Transmission is a five-speed manual with a hydraulic clutch.

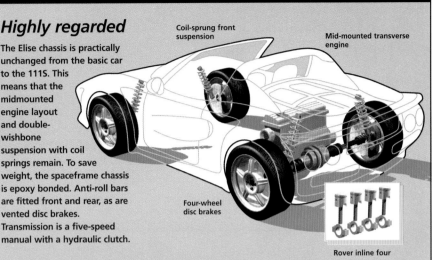

Coil-sprung front suspension

Mid-mounted transverse engine

Four-wheel disc brakes

Rover inline four

THE POWER PACK

Extra VVC power

The main development for the 111S occurs under the bonnet. For the power the chassis craved, Lotus turned to MG and its Rover K-Series VVC 1.8-litre engine, which works well in the successful MGF. VVC stands for Variable Valve Control. This system continuously varies the duration of the intake valve opening and its phasing according to engine speed throughout the rev range. In contrast to Honda's VTEC solution, VVC delivers power smoothly rather than cutting in like a turbo. Thought tengine is all alloy, the 111S still weighs only 71kg (157lbs) more than its smaller-engined sibling.

In demand

The 111S was so eagerly awaited that Lotus can't seem to build enough of them! As a result of this, secondhand examples are rare and command prices that are in the same ball park as a new one. It's hardly a practical family car, but it's amazing fun.

The 111S is the nearest thing to a street-legal go-kart.

Lotus ELISE

You may either love or hate it, but there's no denying the uniqueness of the Elise's styling. In uprated 111S form, Lotus has created one of the most desirable cars in production – a true heir to the original Elan.

Front-end boot

The Elise is not renowned for its practicality. What space is available is used for extra luggage capacity, including a front-end boot into which a few bags of groceries can be squeezed.

Rover K-series engine

Rover's highly acclaimed K-series VVC engine provides the power for the Elise. Midmounted to optimize weight distribution, it has sequential fuel injection and is distributorless.

Unique wheels

The 111S has specially designed six-spoke alloy wheels, and these are the most obvious clue that this is the high-performance version. The wheels also allow for wider rubber to be used: 225s at the back as opposed to 205s on the standard Elise.

Lightweight

A Lotus tradition is lightness, and the Elise follows this line. The spaceframe is constructed in aluminium, which is glued together rather than welded. The whole construction weighs just over 68kg (150lbs), enabling the 111S to have the great power-to-weight ratio of 4.9kg (10.9lbs) per bhp. The acceleration is in supercar territory.

Vented discs

To save yet more weight, vented disc brakes have been used front and rear. There is no servo assistance for either the brakes or the steering.

Close ratios

To exploit the maximum from the Rover engine, Lotus has played with the transmission. Close ratios ensure sensational in-gear acceleration.

Specifications

1999 Lotus Elise 111S

ENGINE
Type: Inline four
Construction: Aluminium block and head
Valve gear: Four valves per cylinder operated by two overhead camshafts
Bore and stroke: 89mm (3.52in) x 90mm (3.57in)
Displacement: 1796cc (110ci)
Compression ratio: 10.5:1
Induction system: Multipoint sequential fuel injection
Maximum power: 143bhp at 7000rpm
Maximum torque: 128lb-ft at 4500rpm
Top Speed: 209km/h (130mph)
0–96km (0–60mph): 5.6 sec

TRANSMISSION
Five-speed manual

BODY/CHASSIS
Aluminium chassis with composite body panels

SPECIAL FEATURES

The rear lights on the Elise are taken from the Toyota parts bin.

Side ducts provide cooling air to the midmounted engine.

RUNNING GEAR
Steering: Rack-and-pinion
Front suspension: Double wishbones with coil springs, telescopic shock absorbers and anti-roll bar
Rear suspension: Double wishbones with coil springs, and telescopic shock absorbers
Brakes: Vented disc, 28.2cm (11.1in) dia. (front and rear)
Wheels: Alloy 5J x 15 (front), 7.5J x 16 (rear)
Tyres: Pirelli 185/55 R15 (front); 225/45 R16 (rear)

DIMENSIONS
Length: 3.7m (146.7in)
Width: 1.72m (68.0in)
Height: 1.2m (47.3in)
Wheelbase: 120cm (90.6in)
Track: 144cm (56.7in) (front), 145cm (57.2in) (rear)
Weight: 770kg (1698lbs)

MGA

The first post-war MG, the MGA, had a slippery aerodynamic body based on a Le Mans racer. It was also reasonably simple, reliable and affordable, plus it had good handling.

"...slide the back."

"The big sprung steering wheel and features like the floor-mounted dip switch tell you the car is old, but once you're on the move the heavy steering lightens up and develops the kind of feel a rack-and-pinion system should. There's adequate power from the ordinary pushrod engine and the ride is better than you expect, but mid-corner bumps catch it out and send you skittering across the road. Particularly with the Twin Cam engine, there's enough power to slide the back end through corners."

Traditional British sports car interior includes large, easy-to-read Smiths gauges and large-diameter sprung steering wheel.

Milestones

1955 MGA introduced
after three EX 182 prototypes do well at Le Mans: one averages 140km/h (87mph) for 24 hours.

1956 Hardtop coupe
follows the original convertible, with larger windshield and wind-up windows.

Second MGA prototype was converted into a record breaker, but proved unsuitable.

1958 MGA Twin Cam
with its larger, 1588cc (97ci) engine gives more performance. It has Lockheed front disc brakes instead of drums, but problems with the engine see compression ratio dropped to 8.3:1.

BMC campaigned the MGA in rallies but was overshadowed by the Austin-Healey 3000.

1959 Engine size of the overhead-valve cars is 1588cc (97ci).

1960 Bodyshells from the discontinued Twin Cam are used for the MGA De Luxe.

1961 MGA MkII
is introduced, but production runs only until 1962.

UNDER THE SKIN

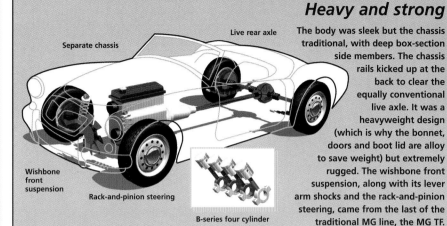

Separate chassis

Live rear axle

Wishbone front suspension

Rack-and-pinion steering

B-series four cylinder

Heavy and strong

The body was sleek but the chassis traditional, with deep box-section side members. The chassis rails kicked up at the back to clear the equally conventional live axle. It was a heavyweight design (which is why the bonnet, doors and boot lid are alloy to save weight) but extremely rugged. The wishbone front suspension, along with its lever arm shocks and the rack-and-pinion steering, came from the last of the traditional MG line, the MG TF.

THE POWER PACK

Pushrod power

As MG was part of BMC (British Motor Corporation), the MGA used the BMC B-series engine, a cast-iron overhead-valve pushrod engine with three main bearings and, originally in the MGA, a displacement of 189cc (91ci). Power for the pushrod B-series ranged from 68bhp for the initial 1489cc (91ci) unit to 86bhp in the final 1622cc (99ci) form. It was a non-crossflow design with carburetors and exhaust on the same side. The engine was strong and reliable. With the twin-cam, alloy head, power was hiked to 108bhp.

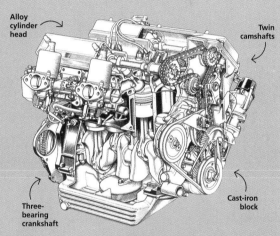

Alloy cylinder head

Twin camshafts

Three-bearing crankshaft

Cast-iron block

Twin Cam

Rarest and most desirable of all MGAs is the Twin Cam, with a B-series block and a new alloy twin-cam head giving 108bhp. Early engines were unreliable if not serviced properly and sales never took off – but now a 'sorted' Twin Cam is very desirable.

The MGA Twin Cam is desirable despite the stories of its unreliability.

MGA

The MGA could hardly fail. It had all the ingredients of the older upright models that came before it – like the TA, TD and TF – but with a body that looked incredibly modern in the mid-1950s.

Optional four-wheel discs

Early MGAs have drum brakes all around. The Twin Cam has front discs, as did all MGAs from 1959. Towards the end of production, you could order four-wheel Dunlop disc brakes if you specified the centre lock wire wheels.

B-series engine

The MGA's predecessor had a 1466cc (89ci) engine, which was replaced for the MGA by the B-series engine, originally in 1489cc (91ci) form.

Optional heater

There is little that is luxurious about the early MGA: even the crude Smiths heater was an option.

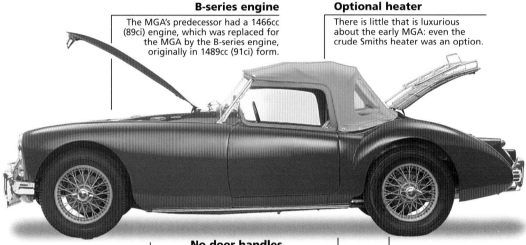

Alloy body panels

To help reduce weight, the bonnet, fenders, doors and boot are all made of aluminium instead of heavy steel.

No door handles

With car theft almost unheard of in the mid-1950s, it was possible to build a car with no external door handles. You simply put your hand through the sliding side window and opened the interior handle. It was also cheaper and gave a cleaner look to the door.

Wire or disc wheels

The MGA could be ordered with either centre lock wire wheels or the more modern looking perforated steel discs.

Live axle

Virtually all sports cars from the 1950s had live rear axles with semi-elliptic leaf springs. This arrangement worked well in the MGA.

Rack-and-pinion steering

Many 1950s British sports cars used advanced (for its time) rack-and-pinion steering.

Different grille

Early MGAs, like this one, have a sloping radiator grille, but for the last of the line, the MkII, the grille bars are inset almost vertically.

Optional axle ratio

If you wanted better acceleration from your MGA, you could order a lower rear axle final drive ratio (4.55:1 compared with 4.10:1).

Specifications
1959 MGA MkI

ENGINE

Type: In-line four cylinder
Construction: Cast-iron block and head
Valve gear: Two in-line valves per cylinder operated by single block-mounted camshaft via pushrods and rockers
Bore and stroke: 75mm (2.96in) x 89mm (3.50in)
Displacement: 1588cc (97ci)
Compression ratio: 8.9:1
Induction system: Two SU H4 carburetors
Maximum power: 80bhp at 5600rpm
Maximum torque: 95lb-ft at 4000rpm
Top Speed: 169km/h (105mph)
0–96km/h (0–60mph): 15.6 seconds

TRANSMISSION

Four-speed manual

BODY/CHASSIS

Separate box-section chassis with steel and alloy two-seater roadster or coupé body

SPECIAL FEATURES

MkI MGAs have upright rear lights mounted on small fender plinths. The MkII is recognizable by its stylish, horizontally mounted rear taillights.

RUNNING GEAR

Steering: Rack-and-pinion
Front suspension: Double wishbones with coil springs and lever arm shocks
Rear suspension: Live axle with semi-elliptic leaf springs and lever arm shocks
Brakes: Discs front, drums rear
Wheels: Centre lock wire spoke or steel discs, 40.6cm (16in) dia.
Tyres: 14.2cm (5.60in) x 40.6cm (16in), crossply

DIMENSIONS

Length: 3.96m (156in)
Width: 1.47m (58in)
Height: 1.27 (50in)
Wheelbase: 239cm (94in)
Track: 120cm (47.5in) (front), 122cm (48.2in) (rear)
Weight: 900kg (1985lbs)

MGB

One of the best-loved sports cars the world has ever known, the MGB also still retains its status as one of the longest-lived. In Roadster form, it quickly became the archetypal British sports car of the postwar era.

"...pure enjoyment."

"In 1962, the MGB was a fine expression of the ideal sports car, and one of the most affordable on the market. The steering is communicative and the handling predictable – at least until you hit a bump, when it gets knocked out of shape all too easily. The B-series engine is tractable from low revs but does not have a high redline. For pure enjoyment, the MGB was hard to beat and it is a fine value today."

The MGB has a classic and simple interior, although the steering wheel seems huge for a sports car by today's standards.

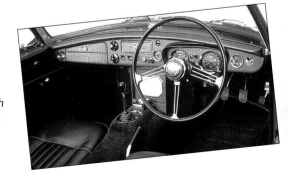

Milestones

1962 After a four-year development period, the MGB Roadster is first shown to the public at the Motor Show at Earl's Court in England.

1963 A fibreglass hardtop becomes a popular and inexpensive option.

The six-cylinder MGC can be recognized by the big bonnet bulge.

1964 The engine receives a five-bearing crankshaft and an oil cooler becomes standard.

1965 The Roadster is joined by a GT coupé model.

The MGB was available in GT and Roadster forms. These are post-1974 'rubber bumper' models.

1967 A new Mk II model receives an all-synchromesh transmission and the option of automatic transmission. The MGB remains in production until 1980.

UNDER THE SKIN

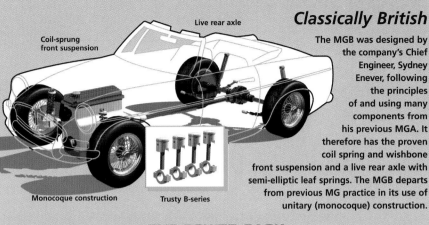

Coil-sprung front suspension

Live rear axle

Monocoque construction

Trusty B-series

Classically British

The MGB was designed by the company's Chief Engineer, Sydney Enever, following the principles of and using many components from his previous MGA. It therefore has the proven coil spring and wishbone front suspension and a live rear axle with semi-elliptic leaf springs. The MGB departs from previous MG practice in its use of unitary (monocoque) construction.

THE POWER PACK

Rugged engine

MG could have opted to fit the powerful 108bhp, twin-cam engine that it had developed for the MGA in the MGB. However, the poor reliability record of this powerplant led to the choice of the well-proven overhead-valve B-series engine. For the MGB, it is bored out to 1796cc (110ci), and power has increased from 86bhp to 95bhp. The bore castings are siamesed and the main bearings beefed up, but the head gear remains as before. One of its best characteristics is a flat torque curve.

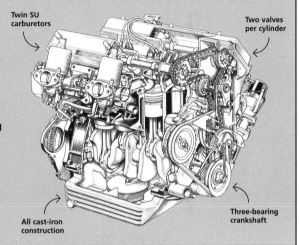

Twin SU carburetors

Two valves per cylinder

All cast-iron construction

Three-bearing crankshaft

Prized original

In MG circles, an early example of the original Roadster with the three-bearing engine is highly desirable. Built for only two years, it is rare to find in good condition and is keenly sought-after. The earliest car represents the purest expression of the MGB form.

The early MGB is a prized collector's car.

MGB

There is no doubt that the MGB is what sports cars are supposed to be like. An open-topped, two-seater, front-engined, rear-wheel drive car is the way to travel.

Monocoque construction

Unlike all previous MG cars, the 'B' was designed around monocoque principles, using strong, double-skinned sills. This simplified the production process, reduced build costs and made the overall package more effective.

Leaf-sprung rear

Although MG experimented with an independently sprung rear end, the MGB has a live rear axle. It is suspended by semi-elliptic leaf springs and uses lever-arm shock absorbers.

Chrome bumpers

Early MGBs are colloquially known as 'chrome bumper' cars to distinguish them from the Federal-equipped 'rubber bumper' cars. Aesthetically, the original chrome finish is more pleasing and retains the familiar slatted grille of the older MGs.

Wind-up windows

Unlike all previous MG sports cars, which stuck with the old British custom of removable side windows or curtains, the MGB has glass windows that are opened and closed using a hand crank. Though this is a matter of course in US-built cars, it's considered a luxury for MG owners.

Specifications

1962 MGB Roadster

ENGINE
Type: In-line four-cylinder
Construction: Cast-iron block and head
Valve gear: Two valves per cylinder operated by a single camshaft via pushrods
Bore and stroke: 80mm (3.16in) x 89mm (3.5in)
Displacement: 1796cc (110ci)
Compression ratio: 8.8:1
Induction system: Two SU carburetors
Maximum power: 95bhp at 5500rpm
Maximum torque: 110lb-ft at 3500rpm
Top Speed: 169km/h (105mph)
0–96km (0–60mph): 12.5 sec

TRANSMISSION
Four-speed manual (overdrive optional)

BODY/CHASSIS
Monocoque chassis with two-door steel open body

SPECIAL FEATURES

The early three-bearing MGB is recognizable by its 'pull' door handles.

The MGB was designed with chrome bumpers, but post-1974 cars have rubber bumpers to meet the US safety regulations.

RUNNING GEAR
Steering: Rack-and-pinion
Front suspension: Wishbones with coil springs and lever-arm shock absorbers
Rear suspension: Live axle with semi-elliptic springs and lever-arm shock absorbers
Brakes: Discs (front), drums (rear)
Wheels: Steel, 35.6cm (14in) dia.
Tyres: 165/70 14

DIMENSIONS
Length: 3.89m (153.2in)
Width: 1.52m (59.9in)
Height: 1.25m (49.4in)
Wheelbase: 231cm (91in)
Track: 125cm (49.2in) (front), 125cm (49.2in) (rear)
Weight: 943kg (2080lbs)

Spacious cabin
By sports car standards, room inside the cockpit is very generous and the driver and passenger have no difficulty getting comfortable.

MG **MAESTRO TURBO**

Advertised as the fastest production MG ever built, the MG Maestro Turbo was also the fastest-accelerating front-wheel drive car in the world at the time of its launch.

"...sheer performance."

"Its boxy shape hides a real performer that's much faster than the VW GTI. It operates best when the engine is spinning near 3000rpm, and full throttle gives acceleration that can surpass several supercars. It will hurtle to 160km/h (100mph) in under 20 seconds. The other surprise is that it doesn't torque steer and is able to corner at very high speeds with very little body roll. The ride is very rigid, but you can forgive that simply for its sheer performance."

The traditional red MG octagonal logo adorns the Maestro's thick-rimmed wheel.

Milestones

1983 Austin Rover
introduces the Maestro range. It has powerplants that range from the 1.3-litres right up to the powerful MG 103-bhp, 1.6-litre engine.

The original 1.6-litre MG Maestro could reach 111mph.

1984 The MG
Maestro gets a larger 2.0-litre engine with 115bhp.

1988 At the British
Motor Show, Austin Rover unveils the fastest Maestro yet, the Turbo. Power goes up to 150bhp. It goes on sale the following year.

There was also a turbocharged MG Montego sedan.

1991 Production
comes to an end after only 505 MG Maestro Turbos have been built.

UNDER THE SKIN

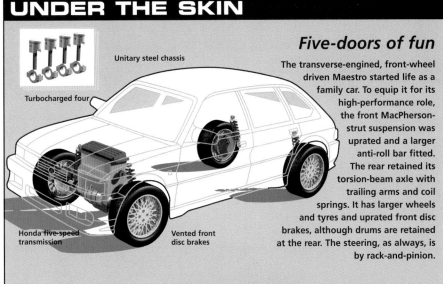

Unitary steel chassis

Turbocharged four

Honda five-speed transmission

Vented front disc brakes

Five-doors of fun

The transverse-engined, front-wheel driven Maestro started life as a family car. To equip it for its high-performance role, the front MacPherson-strut suspension was uprated and a larger anti-roll bar fitted. The rear retained its torsion-beam axle with trailing arms and coil springs. It has larger wheels and tyres and uprated front disc brakes, although drums are retained at the rear. The steering, as always, is by rack-and-pinion.

THE POWER PACK

Turbo four

For the MG Maestro, Austin Rover used its relatively new O-Series 2.0-litre engine. It is a slightly long-stroke inline four-cylinder with a cast-iron block and alloy head. The head holds a single, belt-driven camshaft opening two valves per cylinder. Modern electronic engine management control permits a reasonable 8.5:1 compression ratio to be used with the intercooled Garrett AiResearch T3 turbocharger. Like an Italian high-performance engine, the intake valves are sodium-filled to deal with the extra heat generated from the turbo. Packing 150bhp and 167lb-ft of torque, it made the MG the fastest-accelerating car of its type.

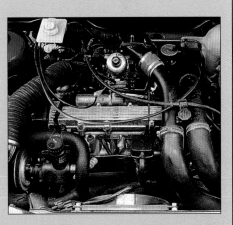

Top turbo

In the 1980s, MG had three turbocharged models – the Metro, Montego and Maestro – which shared the Montego's running gear and engine. All were fast, but the Maestro had the best power-to-weight ratio and therefore the best performance.

The Maestro Turbo remains the fastest-accelerating production MG.

MG **MAESTRO TURBO**

The Maestro was an unlikely high-performance car. There was no money left over for MG to give it a sporty two-door body. But with an abundance of aftermarket parts available, a body kit and alloy wheels would dramatically improve its look.

Rack-and-pinion steering
When the MG Maestro moved from a 1.6- to the 2.0-litre engine, it was given quicker-ratio, power-assisted, rack-and-pinion steering with 2.9 turns lock to lock.

Four-cylinder engine
Maestro Turbos use an engine found in other Austin Rover cars. The 2.0-litre, O-Series unit is a conventional cast-iron block, alloy head, overhead-cam unit with two valves per cylinder.

Low-profile tyres
At 185/55 HR15, the Turbo had lower-profile tyres than almost all its rivals, most of which had 60-section tyres. The lower-profile tyre brings a sharper steering response and better handling because sidewall flex is greatly reduced.

Honda transmission

The high-performance
MG Maestro Turbo
uses a Honda five-
speed transmission.

Mixed shock absorbers

Austin Rover did not feel it necessary to fit
gas-filled shock absorbers at the rear, using
them only for the more heavily loaded
front end.

Garrett turbo

The Garrett AiResearch T3 turbocharger
is the perfect size for the 2.0-litre
Maestro engine. To maximize power,
it makes 10 psi. of boost.

Specifications

1990 MG Maestro Turbo

ENGINE

Type: Inline four-cylinder

Construction: Cast-iron block and alloy head

Valve gear: Two valves per cylinder operated by a single belt-driven overhead camshaft

Bore and stroke: 85mm (3.33in) x 89mm (3.50in)

Displacement: 1994cc (122ci)

Compression ratio: 8.5:1

Induction system: Single ARG carburetor with Garrett T3 turbocharger and intercooler

Maximum power: 150bhp at 5100rpm

Maximum torque: 169lb-ft at 3500rpm

Top Speed: 217km/h (135mph)

0–96km (0–60mph): 6.4 sec

TRANSMISSION

Five-speed manual

BODY/CHASSIS

Unitary monocoque construction with steel five-door hatchback body

SPECIAL FEATURES

The deep front air dam contains extra driving lights for fast night driving.

RUNNING GEAR

Steering: Rack-and-pinion

Front suspension: MacPherson struts with lower control arms, telescopic gas shock absorbers and anti-roll bar

Rear suspension: Torsion beam axle with trailing arms, coil springs, telescopic shock absorbers and anti-roll bar

Brakes: Vented discs (front), drums (rear)

Wheels: Alloy, 12.7cm (5in) x 38.1cm (15in)

Tyres: 185/55 R15

DIMENSIONS

Length: 4m (160.6in)

Width: 1.68m (66.4in)

Height: 1.42m (55.9in)

Wheelbase: 250cm (98.7in)

Track: 148cm (58.3in) (front), 146cm (57.3in) (rear)

Weight: 1116kg (2460lbs)

Rover **MGF**

When Rover revived the MG marque to start manufacture of a sports car after a gap of 15 years, the new car was a world away from the antiquated but well-loved MGB. It was much more powerful, mid-engined, fast and nimble, and an instant success.

"...quiet and sophisticated."

"The MG sports car has come a long way from the days of the MGB. The MGF is so comfortable, quiet and sophisticated that it seems like a totally different type of car. The mid-engined layout gives tremendous balance, and the unusual Hydragas suspension gives unrivalled comfort and control for a sports car of this type. If driven fast on twisty country roads, the MG is hard to catch and faster than more expensive rivals like the popular BMW Z3."

MGF is well-equipped and comfortable. The Alex Moulton-designed Hydragas suspension gives an unbelievably good ride.

Milestones

1985 MG exhibits the EX-E at the Frankfurt Show to gauge enthusiasm for a future MG. The mid-engined EX-E is not intended for production, but a positive response helps start the project to make a modern MG.

MG RV8 was little more than a re-engineered MGB.

1989 The new MG project team start work.

Styling sketch shows familiar MGF lines that were to come.

1992 The MG RV8 is launched. It's an updated MGB with the 190bhp 3.9-liter version of the Rover V8 engine. It is a very low volume production car simply intended to keep the MG name alive.

1995 Rover chose the Geneva Show to unveil the new MGF. It goes on sale in two versions, a standard 1.8 and a 1.8 VVC with more power thanks to the variable valve control.

UNDER THE SKIN

Gas suspension

The MGF's suspension is what really sets it apart from its rivals. It uses the Hydragas system, which replaces conventional steel springs with gas-filled 'springs' that are interconnected front and rear and work by twin wishbones on all four wheels. Separate shocks and anti-roll bars are used, although the system could be developed to work without them.

Convertible or hardtop

Mid-mounted engine

Steel monocoque

Hydragas suspension

K-Series in-line four

THE POWER PACK

Twin overhead camshafts

Four valves per cylinder

Hydraulic lifters

Variable valve timing

Alloy block and cylinder head

Clever K-Series

The K-Series four-valve-per-cylinder twin cams used in the MG are Rover's most modern design. All alloy, they are light, very compact, have a novel 'sandwich' construction and hydraulic lifters. The extremely sophisticated variable valve arrangement in the VVC engine continuously varies the intake cam timing, keeping the intake valves open longer beyond 4000rpm, to produce more power at high rpm.

Two versions

Two versions of the same engine give a very different feel to the car. The clever variable valve control VVC has much more power, but at higher rpm with 143bhp at 7000rpm rather than the standard car's 118bhp at 5500rpm. There's more torque too, but only by a fraction and again at far higher rpm, so the 1.8 is not the poor relation it seems.

Both 1.8i and VVC models are very entertaining for the money.

Rover **MGF**

The MGF 1.8 VVC is the first MG road car to be rear-engined and front-wheel driven. It is one of the most powerful 1.8-litre cars built, with performance and handling to match.

MG front

Early styling proposals of the MGF were rejected because they did not immediately look like MGs, and so the MGF carries a traditional MG grille.

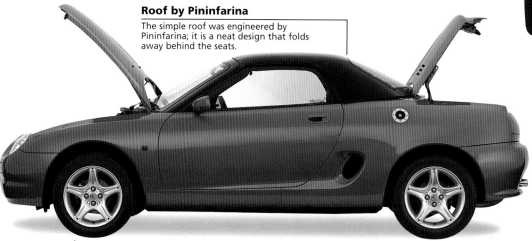

Roof by Pininfarina

The simple roof was engineered by Pininfarina; it is a neat design that folds away behind the seats.

Anti-lock brakes

The more expensive and more powerful VVC model has anti-lock brakes as a standard feature. They are an option on the standard 1.8 model.

Engine air intake

Air for the engine is drawn in through two ducts just ahead of the rear wheel arches.

Mid engine

The stretched Rover engine is mounted transversely, making it the first mid-engined MG road car. The engine is revolutionary in having a water jacket of less than 38mm (1.5in) around its cylinders to cool them.

Electric steering

The power steering for the MGF comes from a small electric motor rather than the traditional engine-driven hydraulic pump.

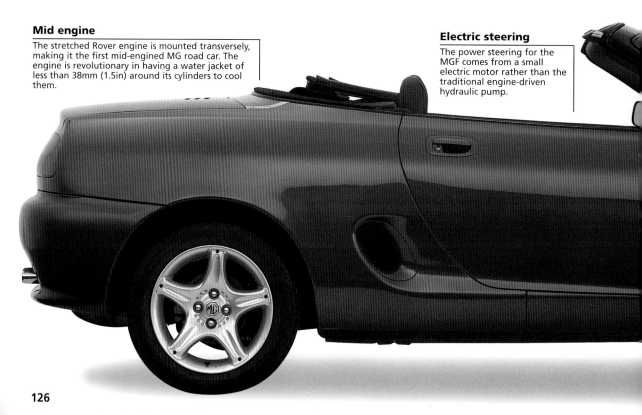

Front radiator

Although the engine is behind the cockpit, the radiator is in the traditional place at the front, exposed to a greater airflow than it would be next to the engine.

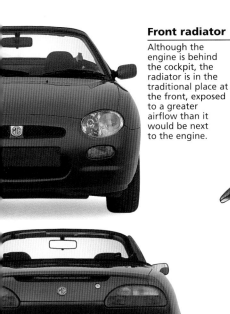

Twin exhausts

Although the engine is only a four cylinder, the MGF has twin exhaust pipes, like the MR-2, to balance the appearance of the rear end.

Hydragas springs

Pressurized gas replaces conventional coil springs. It's a refined version of the Hydragas system that Rover first used more than 10 years ago.

Specifications

1996 Rover MGF VVC

ENGINE

Type: In-line four-cylinder twin cam
Construction: Alloy block, head and sump with cast-iron wet liners
Valve gear: Four valves per cylinder operated by twin overhead camshafts with variable valve timing for the intake valves
Bore and stroke: 80mm (3.15in) x 89mm (3.5in)
Displacement: 1796cc (110ci)
Compression ratio: 10.5:1
Induction system: Rover MEMS electronic fuel injection
Maximum power: 143bhp at 7000rpm
Maximum torque: 128lb-ft at 4500rpm
Top Speed: 211km/h (131mph)
0–96km (0–60mph): 7.8 sec

TRANSMISSION

Five-speed manual

BODY/CHASSIS

Two-door, two seat convertible with steel monocoque chassis

SPECIAL FEATURES

MGF's K-Series engine sees the pioneering use of plastic for the intake manifold.

Retro-styled fuel filler cap shows the link to older MGs.

RUNNING GEAR

Steering: Rack-and-pinion
Front suspension: Twin wishbones, Hydragas springs, telescopic shocks and anti-roll bar
Rear suspension: Twin wishbones, Hydragas springs, telescopic shocks and anti-roll bar
Brakes: Ventilated discs (front), 24cm (9.45in) dia, solid discs (rear), 24cm (9.45in) dia.
Wheels/tyres: Alloy 16.5cm (6.5in) x 38.1cm (15in) with 205/50 VR15 tyres

DIMENSIONS

Length: 3.9m (154in)
Width: 1.77m (70in)
Height: 1.27m (50in)
Wheelbase: 238cm (93.5in)
Track: 142cm (56in) (front), 141cm (55.5in) (rear)
Weight: 1121kg (2471lbs)

Morgan **SUPER SPORTS**

The Morgan was the most popular three-wheeler ever, and was produced for more than 40 years. It served as inexpensive transportation, but people quickly became aware of its performance possibilities: even today, tuned versions can beat four-wheeled cars in vintage racing.

"...a wheel is missing."

"The Morgan's cockpit is very narrow, but you're totally in tune with your surroundings. It's not easy to drive at first, with a hand throttle instead of a foot pedal, wide-spaced gears and high-ratio steering. However, you soon learn to enjoy the acceleration and acquire the art of steering the car on the throttle. It hops and skips over bumpy surfaces and darts quickly around fast corners, but it's surprisingly stable considering that a wheel is missing."

A cramped cockpit and minimal weather protection don't spoil the driving experience.

Milestones

1910 H.F.S. Morgan launches his first JAP-engined three-wheeler.

The earlier three-wheelers had almost no sporty pretensions.

1912 A Morgan wins at the first-ever cyclecar meeting at Brooklands.

1928 The Super Sports model arrives. It has lower bodywork and a rounded tail.

Morgan is better known for its long-lived four-wheeler models.

1935 As Morgan branches out into four-wheelers, it launches the Ford-engined F-Type.

1952 The very last F-Type Morgan is produced, as the company devotes its attention to four-wheelers.

UNDER THE SKIN

Burman steering

Twin-tube chassis

Sliding-pillar front suspension

Simplicity

Reflecting its original role as a bargain cyclecar, the Morgan is simply engineered but effective. The chassis is a twin-tube arrangement, with one of the tubes acting as an exhaust pipe on early models. At the front end is Morgan's sliding-pillar suspension, which is still used today, and there is a swinging fork and leaf springs at the rear – effectively independent suspension for all three wheels. Power goes through a driveshaft and chain with a three-speed manual transmission.

Classic V-twin

THE POWER PACK

Brought-in power

Morgan trikes came with a variety of engines over the years, from single-cylinders to flat-fours. The classic powerplant has always been an exposed V-twin engine; the most notable was the JAP. Early engines were air-cooled, later ones water-cooled. The seminal Super Sports most commonly used a V-twin by JAP or Matchless, which was used in many motorcycles of the period. Other engine brands that have been used include MAG, Blackburn, Anzani and Precision. From 1935, there was also the option of the Ford Model Y four-cylinder side-valve engine.

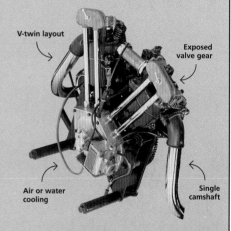

V-twin layout

Exposed valve gear

Air or water cooling

Single camshaft

Sport legend

Morgans came in many varieties, from cost-effective runabouts through family transporters to competition racers. The most highly regarded are the Super Sports models, with their low-slung bodies, motorcycle fenders and barrel-back bodywork.

Three-wheeler Morgans have a devoted following.

Morgan SUPER SPORTS

Three-wheelers may have begun life as a low priced, simple solution to getting about, but Morgan refined the breed. Some reached speeds as high as 209km/h (130mph) and became track legends.

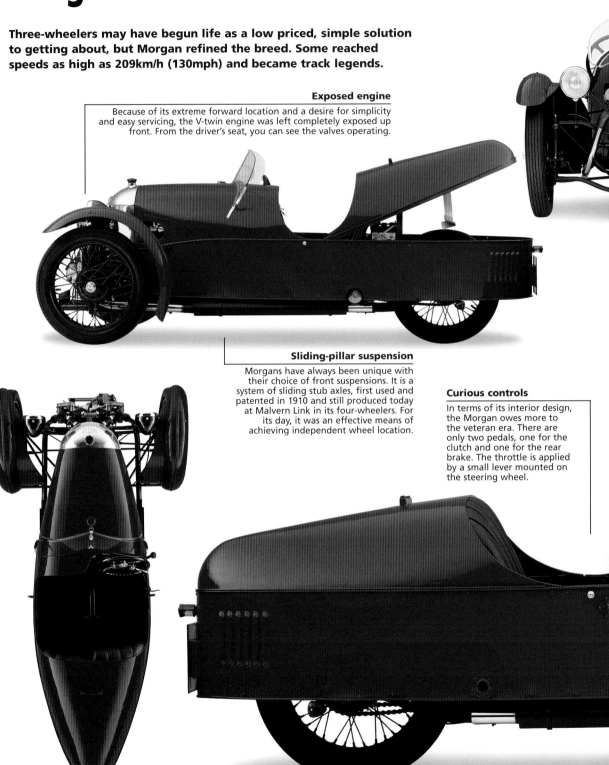

Exposed engine
Because of its extreme forward location and a desire for simplicity and easy servicing, the V-twin engine was left completely exposed up front. From the driver's seat, you can see the valves operating.

Sliding-pillar suspension
Morgans have always been unique with their choice of front suspensions. It is a system of sliding stub axles, first used and patented in 1910 and still produced today at Malvern Link in its four-wheelers. For its day, it was an effective means of achieving independent wheel location.

Curious controls
In terms of its interior design, the Morgan owes more to the veteran era. There are only two pedals, one for the clutch and one for the rear brake. The throttle is applied by a small lever mounted on the steering wheel.

Prop-and-chain drive

Drive is taken from the front engine to the rear wheel initially with a driveshaft to the transmission. Drive then goes to the wheel using a simple chain and sprocket.

Lever operated front brakes

The majority of 'ordinary' Morgans had only one brake, a 'band' brake mounted on the rear hub. As an option – but standard on the rapid Super Sports – front drum brakes were fitted. These are operated by cable and handbrake on the outside of the car.

Single rear wheel

In terms of stability, a single rear wheel is superior to a single front wheel. Because it has only three wheels, the design is simple (as no differential is necessary) and weight is kept down, allowing the Morgan to perform far better than its modest power output suggests.

Choice of rear-end treatment

Two different rear end styles were offered by Morgan for the Super Sports. The first was a rounded back, but equally popular was the so-called 'barrel back' design.

Specifications

1932 Morgan Super Sports

ENGINE

Type: V-twin

Construction: Cast-iron block and heads

Valve gear: Two valves per cylinder operated by a single camshaft via pushrods and rockers

Bore and stroke: 86mm (3.37in) x 86mm (3.37in)

Displacement: 990cc (60ci)

Compression ratio: 7.5:1

Induction system: Single Amal carburetor

Maximum power: 39bhp at 4200rpm

Maximum torque: 50lb-ft at 2400rpm

Top Speed: 137km/h (85mph)

0–96km (0–60mph): 14 sec

TRANSMISSION

Three-speed manual

BODY/CHASSIS

Separate thin-tube chassis with doorless steel sports body

SPECIAL FEATURES

The rear body lifts up for easy access to the rear suspension and drivetrain.

The handbrake lever is mounted outside the body.

RUNNING GEAR

Steering: Burman

Front suspension: Sliding stub axles with coil springs and shock absorbers

Rear suspension: Pivoting fork with quarter-elliptic springs and shock absorbers

Brakes: Drums (front and rear)

Wheels: Wire, 45.7cm (18in) dia.

Tyres: 4.00 x 18

DIMENSIONS

Length: 3.15m (124in)

Width: 1.5m (59.0in)

Height: 1m (40.0in)

Wheelbase: 216cm (85.0in)

Track: 126cm (49.5in) (front)

Weight: 4433kg (954lbs)

Morris **MINOR**

Germany had its VW Beetle, but Great Britain had the Morris Minor. As a true people's car, it was well-designed, dependable and affordable. For years, it was a best-seller and still has a passionate following today.

"...way above the norm."

"In its day, the Minor was a revelation to drive, and it still has the potential to surprise you. No other economy car had such a balanced chassis, which, to this day, is fun to drive and at the same time offers an uncommonly good ride. The MM's sidevalve engine is its Achilles' heel, thanks to lazy response and poor refinement. Later Minors, with the pushrod, overhead-valve A-series engines, had much more throttle response."

Morris kept things clean and simple inside, but it suited the Minor's character perfectly.

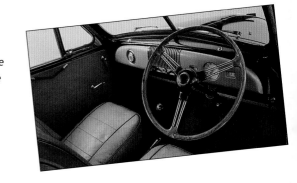

Milestones

1948 Alec Issigonis' dazzling new Minor is launched in two-door sedan and convertible forms to rave reviews.

Later models are still plentiful, but the first MM is now a rarity.

1952 Following the merger of Austin and Morris to form BMC, the old sidevalve engine is replaced by Austin's 803cc (49ci) overhead-valve unit.

1953 The first Traveller station wagon is completed.

1956 The Minor 1000 arrives, with a 948cc (58ci) engine, better transmission and an updated interior.

The convertible was as much of a hit as the sedan and is now the most collectible Minor.

1971 After more than two decades, often as Britain's best-selling car, the Minor is finally withdrawn from sales.

UNDER THE SKIN

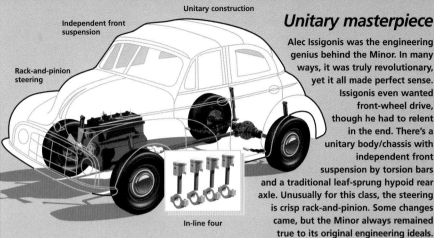

Unitary construction

Independent front suspension

Rack-and-pinion steering

In-line four

Unitary masterpiece

Alec Issigonis was the engineering genius behind the Minor. In many ways, it was truly revolutionary, yet it all made perfect sense. Issigonis even wanted front-wheel drive, though he had to relent in the end. There's a unitary body/chassis with independent front suspension by torsion bars and a traditional leaf-sprung hypoid rear axle. Unusually for this class, the steering is crisp rack-and-pinion. Some changes came, but the Minor always remained true to its original engineering ideals.

THE POWER PACK

Morris cedes to Austin

Designer Alec Issigonis wanted to use a new flat-four engine in the Minor, but economics forced Morris to depend on its prewar Series E sidevalve 918cc (56ci) engine, which was underpowered (at 28bhp) and lethargic. When Morris and Austin merged, it was natural that Austin's superior A30 overhead-valve 803cc (49ci) engine should be substituted. It revs better and gives a faster top speed. That engine grew to 948cc (58ci) and 37bhp in 1956 (in the definitive Minor 1000), and finally to 1098cc (67ci) and 48bhp in 1962.

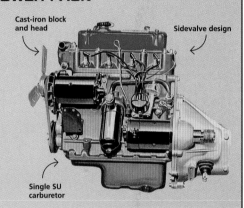

Cast-iron block and head

Sidevalve design

Single SU carburetor

Tourer or woody?

The pick of the Minor family is the convertible version, called the Tourer, although the 'woody' Traveller station wagon is highly prized. The Tourer has a typical 1950s English charm about it and a well-designed soft top. In general, the earlier the model, the more precious it is, so MM Tourers are the most highly collectible of all Morris Minors.

Wooden panels on the Traveller help make it a collector's favourite.

Morris **MINOR**

The chubby styling of the Minor became very familiar on British roads as the population took to the charms of this competent little car. It offered a level of driving pleasure unseen before in its class.

Unibody construction

In 1948, just about every car had a separate chassis. The Minor was way ahead of its time in adopting unitary construction. The floor was produced in a single pressing, cutting costs and keeping weight down. It was rigid, too, as proven by the convertible, which didn't need very much body reinforcement.

Sidevalve engine

The first Minors used an outdated Morris sidevalve engine to keep costs down. Issigonis had developed new flat-four sidevalve engines, but these were shelved. A more satisfying Austin A30 overhead-valve engine arrived in 1952.

Correct proportions

One of the Minor's main selling points was that it looked right, even though Morris' boss called the prototype a 'poached egg.' One famous story relates how Issigonis, at the eleventh hour, sawed a prototype in half along its length, widening the shell by 10cm (4in) until, in the charming words of an official press release, 'proportion was propitiated and harmony satisfied.'

Basic trim

The Minor was deliberately sparsely equipped. Only the driver's door has a lock, for example, and the rear windows are fixed in position. Inside, the dashboard is plain painted metal.

Low-set headlights

In an age when many cars still had separate headlights, the faired-in, very low-set lights were a startling detail. They give the body a smooth, air-formed look. They were raised after 1950.

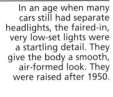

Specifications

1949 Morris Minor MM

ENGINE

Type: In-line four-cylinder
Construction: Cast-iron block and head
Valve gear: Two side-mounted valves per cylinder
Bore and stroke: 59mm (2.24in) x 90mm (3.54in)
Displacement: 918cc (56ci)
Compression ratio: 6.7:1
Induction system: Single SU carburetor
Maximum power: 28bhp at 4400rpm
Maximum torque: 39lb-ft at 2400rpm
Top Speed: 103km/h (64mph)
0–96km/h (0–60mph): N/A

TRANSMISSION

Four-speed manual

BODY/CHASSIS

Unitary monocoque construction with steel two-door sedan body

SPECIAL FEATURES

Trafficators, as they were called, were fitted on British cars, although the US market got flashing directional lights.

The split windshield reflects the era when curved glass was still a technical challenge to manufacture.

RUNNING GEAR

Steering: Rack-and-pinion
Front suspension: Wishbones with torsion bars and shock absorbers
Rear suspension: Live axle with semi-elliptic leaf springs and shock absorbers
Brakes: Drums (front and rear)
Wheels: Steel, 35.6cm (14in) dia.
Tyres: 5.00 x 14

DIMENSIONS

Length: 3.76m (148.0in)
Width: 1.55m (61.0in)
Height: 1.45m (57.0in)
Wheelbase: 218cm (86.0in)
Track: 128cm (50.5in) (front), 128cm (50.5in)(rear)
Weight: 792kg (1745lbs)

Reliant SCIMITAR

Reliant bought an Ogle-styled body and mated it to the Sabre Six chassis and running gear. The result was the handsome Scimitar, which proved to be a fast and competent grand tourer.

"...fast, relaxed cruising."

"There's no shortage of performance here – the Scimitar will see you through the ¼-mile in an impressive 17.0 seconds and on to a genuine 193km/h (120mph). It was designed to provide fast, relaxed cruising, with high gearing and overdrive making the most of the very torquey V6 engine. It can be thrown around corners, too, even if it is not the most agile of sportsters. It has the feel of a solid, heavy car."

Reliant took care to emphasize the Scimitar's sporty nature on the inside as well as on the outside of the car.

Milestones

1964 Appropriately, the London Motor Show is chosen for the Scimitar's debut. It has a stunning David Ogle-designed body on a Sabre Six chassis and a Ford engine.

1965 A trailing-arm rear suspension improves handling considerably.

The Scimitar uses underpinnings from the previous Sabre Six.

1966 The SE4b model arrives with a stiffened chassis, a 3.0-litre Ford 'Essex' V6 engine with 146bhp, and steel disc wheels.

The final Scimitar was the GTE SE6, built from 1975 to 1986.

1968 A new Scimitar, the GTE, is unveiled. It is an instant success.

1970 Production of the original Scimitar SE comes to an end. The GTE lasts until 1986. A convertible is launched in 1980.

UNDER THE SKIN

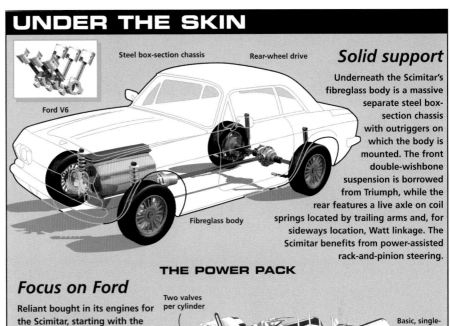

Steel box-section chassis · Rear-wheel drive

Ford V6

Fibreglass body

Solid support

Underneath the Scimitar's fibreglass body is a massive separate steel box-section chassis with outriggers on which the body is mounted. The front double-wishbone suspension is borrowed from Triumph, while the rear features a live axle on coil springs located by trailing arms and, for sideways location, Watt linkage. The Scimitar benefits from power-assisted rack-and-pinion steering.

THE POWER PACK

Focus on Ford

Reliant bought in its engines for the Scimitar, starting with the straight-six from the Ford Zephyr. In 1966, the Ford Essex 3.0-litre V6 became available, turning the Scimitar into a very competent machine. It is an uncomplicated, all-iron, pushrod single-cam engine with two valves per cylinder. Its long stroke design gives it 146bhp and a credible 172lb-ft of torque. Later Scimitar SE6s were fitted with the smaller 2.8-litre 'Cologne' V6 from 1979.

Two valves per cylinder

Basic, single-cam design

All-iron construction

Six-cylinder block

Glass act

The first hint of what was to become the GTE came with the one-of-a-kind 1966 Ogle and Triplex GTS. The work of Ogle Design, a larger station wagon-type back was fitted to a Scimitar GT to prove what could be done with the then-new Triplex glass. On the production GT, with less glass area, the roofline looked a lot lower, giving the GTE a sporty look.

The Triplex GTS was the forerunner for the production GTE.

Reliant **SCIMITAR**

It was the right blend of perfectly balanced styling, a tough engine and running gear combined with excellent performance that produced a hit for Reliant and an inspiration to other manufacturers.

Ford engine
Ford's Essex V6 engine was first used in the Ford Zephyr in the mid-1960s. Fitting it into the Scimitar transformed the car into a serious performance machine.

Extra stiffening
Because the V6 had considerably more power than the old in-line unit, alterations to the chassis were required in order to prevent flex. The solution was to fit extra bracing between the front and rear suspension assemblies.

Fibreglass body
Fibreglass was used for the body because it was better suited to low-volume production, dispensing with the need for expensive dies.

Handsome styling
The original shape was penned by David Ogle Design and used a Sabre Six chassis. Reliant had the foresight to buy the production tooling for use on its new grand tourer car.

Parts-bin suspension

Scimitars use the double wishbone front suspension from the Triumph TR4 sports car but with different spring rates.

Separate chassis

Scimitars are mounted on a cruciform chassis made from steel box sections, with outriggers running from the main longitudinal chassis rails to the sides of the car.

Live axle

All Scimitars have traditional live axles rather than independent rear suspension. Sideways location is improved by a Watt linkage.

Specifications

1968 Reliant Scimitar SE4b

ENGINE
Type: V6

Construction: Cast-iron block and heads

Valve gear: Two valves per cylinder operated by single camshafts with pushrods and rockers

Bore and stroke: 92mm (3.62in) x 73mm (2.87in)

Displacement: 2994cc (183ci)

Compression ratio: 8.9:1

Induction system: Single downdraft carburetor

Maximum power: 146bhp at 5000rpm

Maximum torque: 172lb-ft at 3000rpm

Top Speed: 193km/h (120mph)

0–96km (0–60mph): 8.8 sec

TRANSMISSION
Four-speed manual

BODY/CHASSIS
Separate box-section steel cruciform chassis with fibreglass two-door coupe body

SPECIAL FEATURES

A racing-style quick-release fuel cap is a unique and interesting touch on what is a low-volume production GT.

All Scimitars have quad circular headlights regardless of model.

RUNNING GEAR
Steering: Rack-and-pinion

Front suspension: Double wishbones with coil springs, telescopic shock absorbers and anti-roll bar

Rear suspension: Live axle with trailing arms, Watt linkage, coil springs and telescopic shock absorbers

Brakes: Drums (front and rear)

Wheels: Steel discs, 12.7cm (5in) x 35.6cm (14in)

Tyres: 185/70-14

DIMENSIONS
Length: 4.3m (170.2in)

Width: 1.65m (65.0in)

Height: 1.33m (52.5in)

Wheelbase: 165cm (65.0in)

Track: 141cm (55.6in) (front), 135cm (53.3in) (rear)

Weight: 1158kg (2554 lbs)

Rolls-Royce **SILVER GHOST**

For a time, the Silver Ghost truly was the best car in the world for those rich enough to afford Rolls-Royce's supreme craftsmanship, unbeatable reliability and high-class image. In fact, it was so good that it remained in production for nearly 20 years in various forms.

"...total mechanical harmony."

"Although the 75bhp of the Alpine Eagle-type Silver Ghost doesn't sound like much, it's enough to take it past 129km/h (80mph), where it can cruise all day. Unlike more modern Rolls-Royces, it's agile too – with just one and a quarter turns of the steering wheel from lock to lock, the Ghost will take even sharp corners with ease. One of the biggest surprises is the effortlessness with which it moves, every part working in total mechanical harmony. The transmission requires practice, but in a Ghost you hardly need to change gears."

Silver coachwork and its whispering quietness gave the Silver Ghost its name.

Milestones

1906 First 40/50 series cars are unveiled – the 13th example is the original Silver Ghost.

1909 The Ghost's engine is enlarged from 7036cc (429ci) to 7428cc (453ci), increasing power output from 48bhp to 60bhp.

All Silver Ghosts have coachbuilt bodies like this 1910 Roi des Belges.

1911 A special Silver Ghost drives from London to Edinburgh in top gear only, with a top speed of 126km/h (78mph), resulting in the London-to-Edinburgh model.

1913 Success in the immensely difficult Alpine Trial leads to the sporty, open four-seater Alpine Eagle model.

1918 Following World War I, Silver Ghosts are made under license in Springfield, Illinois.

1923 The Silver Ghost is finally given a brake servo, the type designed and used for years by rivals Hispano-Suiza.

1925 Silver Ghost production ends.

UNDER THE SKIN

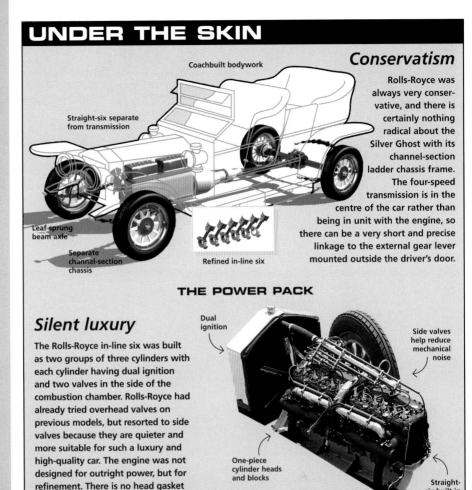

Coachbuilt bodywork

Straight-six separate from transmission

Leaf sprung beam axle

Separate channel-section chassis

Refined in-line six

Conservatism

Rolls-Royce was always very conservative, and there is certainly nothing radical about the Silver Ghost with its channel-section ladder chassis frame. The four-speed transmission is in the centre of the car rather than being in unit with the engine, so there can be a very short and precise linkage to the external gear lever mounted outside the driver's door.

THE POWER PACK

Silent luxury

The Rolls-Royce in-line six was built as two groups of three cylinders with each cylinder having dual ignition and two valves in the side of the combustion chamber. Rolls-Royce had already tried overhead valves on previous models, but resorted to side valves because they are quieter and more suitable for such a luxury and high-quality car. The engine was not designed for outright power, but for refinement. There is no head gasket because cylinder head and block are cast in one piece.

Dual ignition

Side valves help reduce mechanical noise

One-piece cylinder heads and blocks

Straight-six built in two blocks of three cylinders

Real Ghost

There is only one real Silver Ghost: the famous all-silver car, which still exists was the 13th car in the 40/50 series and built in 1907. Soon people were calling all the 40/50 cars Silver Ghosts – it was never an official model name, but has since become the generic term for this model.

Only the 13th 40/50 built can be described as the real Silver Ghost.

Rolls-Royce **SILVER GHOST**

For a Rolls-Royce, the Silver Ghost was amazingly versatile. It could carry stately formal bodywork in near silence, beat all comers in demanding Alpine Trials competitions and even perform as an armoured car in World War I.

Solid axle

Like all cars of its era, the Silver Ghost has a solid front axle. In this case, it is an 'I' section beam mounted on semi-elliptic leaf springs.

Side-valve engine

There are different types of side-valve engines. The Silver Ghost's is an L-head – the valves are along one side of the engine with their heads upward operating in the combustion chambers above them.

Alpine Eagle bodywork

Silver Ghosts carry a diverse range of bodies. This is the open Alpine Eagle style as used in the 1913 Alpine Trial.

Cantilever rear springs

Rolls-Royce changed the rear suspension design several times, settling on a system of cantilevered semi-elliptic rear springs.

Alloy pistons

Although heavy iron pistons were common before World War I, Rolls-Royce used lighter alloy pistons, which eased the stress on the crankshaft and its bearings.

Four-speed transmission

The Ghost's engine has a huge torque output, but the Alpine Eagle model has a four-speed transmission. This way, owners would not be embarrassed by steep mountain passes as they could be with the previous three-speed model.

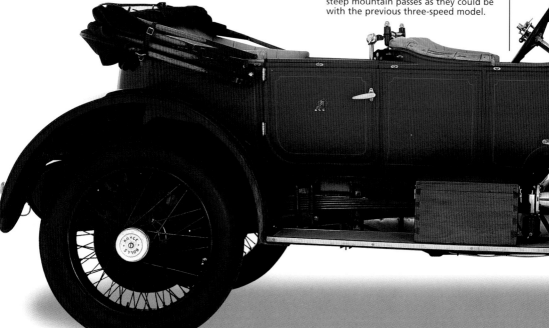

No front brakes

For most of its life, the Silver Ghost had no front brakes, even when some rivals like Hispano-Suiza had switched to four-wheel brakes.

Solid nickel plating

It is no wonder the finish on Rolls-Royces is durable. Nickel plate was applied in thin layers that were soldered to the metal underneath.

Specifications
1913 Rolls-Royce Silver Ghost Alpine Eagle

ENGINE

Type: In-line six-cylinder side-valve
Construction: Cast-iron monoblock with alloy crankcase and pistons
Valve gear: Two side valves per cylinder operated by single gear-driven camshaft
Bore and stroke: 114mm (4.49in) x 121mm (4.76in)
Displacement: 7428cc (453ci)
Compression ratio: 3.5:1
Induction system: Single Rolls-Royce twin-jet carburetor
Maximum power: 75bhp at 1800rpm
Maximum torque: Not quoted
Top Speed: 132km/h (82mph)
0–96km/h (0–60mph): Not quoted

TRANSMISSION

Separate four-speed gearbox

BODY/CHASSIS

Ladder-type steel frame with crossmembers and customer's choice of coachbuilt bodywork

SPECIAL FEATURES

There are two sets of spark plugs. One set runs off a trembler coil system, the other by magneto.

The Spirit of Ecstasy mascot was modelled after motoring pioneer Lord Montagu's secretary, Eleanor Thornton.

RUNNING GEAR

Steering: Worm and nut
Front suspension: Beam axle with semi-elliptic leaf springs
Rear suspension: Live axle with cantilevered semi-elliptic leaf springs
Brakes: Rear drums only, rod operated
Wheels: 88.9cm (35in) wire spoked
Tyres: Dunlop grooved square tread beaded edge 895 x 195

DIMENSIONS

Length: 4.88m (192in)
Width: 4.12m (162.5in)
Height: 4.08m (161in)
Wheelbase: 364cm (143.5in)
Track: 142cm (56in) (front and rear)
Weight: 1295kg (2856lbs) (chassis only)

Rover **P5B**

Rover pulled off quite a coup when it bought the rights to an all-alloy Buick V8 engine. Its first use was in the ageing P5 sedan, a car that became one of the most majestic cars that Rover has ever built.

"...refined good taste."

"A gentleman's carriage would be a correct description for the sophisticated P5B. The seats have the feel of luxury leather armchairs, and the wood panelling suggests refined good taste. The alloy V8 engine and automatic transmission are perfectly matched. The P5B is most at home cruising on the highway. On twisty roads, it really shows its age as the car rolls through the turns. However, the tyres do grip confidently."

P5Bs have traditional British interiors. Sliding behind the wheel gives a feeling of confidence.

Milestones

1958 Rover first launches its 3.0-liter model, codenamed the P5. It bears similar styling to the P4, but is larger and heavier. It is also the first Rover to adopt unitary construction.

1962 A four-door coupé bodyshell with a lower roof line joins the sedan. It proves to be a real success.

The P4 had much more restrained upright styling than the P5.

1967 The P5 range is replaced by the P5B, which is the first model to use the Buick V8 engine, Rostyle steel wheels and front foglights.

1973 The P5B is retired with no direct successor.

The P6 was available with four-cylinder engines as well as the V8.

UNDER THE SKIN

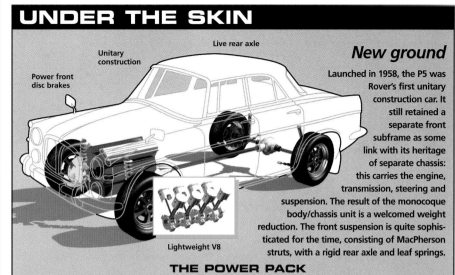

Power front disc brakes

Unitary construction

Live rear axle

Lightweight V8

New ground

Launched in 1958, the P5 was Rover's first unitary construction car. It still retained a separate front subframe as some link with its heritage of separate chassis: this carries the engine, transmission, steering and suspension. The result of the monocoque body/chassis unit is a welcomed weight reduction. The front suspension is quite sophisticated for the time, consisting of MacPherson struts, with a rigid rear axle and leaf springs.

THE POWER PACK

Buick V8

When Rover's managing director, William Martin Hurst, came across an aluminium V8 engine while visiting the US, he was curious. Hurst found out that this was a 3523cc (215ci) Buick unit, offered in the early 1960s Skylark compact. Rover saw it as an ideal replacement for the ageing 3.0-litre engine used in the Rover P5. In 1965, Buick duly granted a licence for Rover to build it. Rover changed the casting process, designed a new intake manifold and fitted twin SU carburetors. In the P5B, it produces 161bhp.

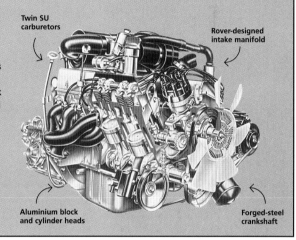

Twin SU carburetors

Rover-designed intake manifold

Aluminium block and cylinder heads

Forged-steel crankshaft

P5B Coupé

Two body styles were offered on the luxurious P5B: a standard sedan and the Coupé. Despite its name, the latter is also a four-door, but has a lower roof line which makes it look more sporty. Enthusiasts tend to prefer the Coupé, but any P5B is value for money.

Today, these stately old Rovers have a loyal enthusiast following.

Rover **P5B**

Installing a V8 engine into the P5 transformed it from a stuffy sedan into a powerful and refined luxury cruiser. Though still considered small, especially for a four door, it proved to be popular in many other markets.

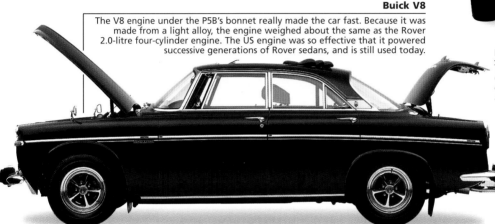

Buick V8

The V8 engine under the P5B's bonnet really made the car fast. Because it was made from a light alloy, the engine weighed about the same as the Rover 2.0-litre four-cylinder engine. The US engine was so effective that it powered successive generations of Rover sedans, and is still used today.

Front disc brakes

The P5B uses front disc brakes to stop its considerable weight at high speeds.

Front subframe

A separate box-section steel subframe carries the engine and suspension. This whole unit can be dropped out for easy servicing, by simply detaching six rubber bushings.

Sumptuous interior

The leather-trimmed seats in the P5B are deeply padded and very comfortable. Cabin ambience is created by plush carpeting, extensive wood veneer trim, chrome detailing and surprisingly modern-looking instruments set right in front of the driver.

Coupé shape

Two inches lower than the P5B sedans, the Coupé has steeper front and rear pillars. It was originally intended to have been a pillarless design, but wind noise and torsional rigidity problems prevented this design.

Power steering

Although optional on the original P5, power steering was a standard item on the V8-engined P5B. This helps when maneuvering the hefty barge at low speeds.

Laminated torsion bars

Rover's choice of laminated torsion bars was very unusual. The advantage of using them was to save valuable space underneath.

Specifications

1971 Rover 3.5-litre P5B Coupé

ENGINE

Type: V8

Construction: Aluminium block and heads

Valve gear: Two valves per cylinder operated by a single camshaft via pushrods and rockers

Bore and stroke: 89mm (3.50in) x 71mm (2.79in)

Displacement: 3528cc (215ci)

Compression ratio: 10.5:1

Induction system: Two SU carburetors

Maximum power: 161bhp at 5200rpm

Maximum torque: 210lb-ft at 2600rpm

Top Speed: 177km/h (110mph)

0–96km (0–60mph): 12.4 sec

TRANSMISSION

Three-speed automatic

BODY/CHASSIS

Integral chassis with four-door steel coupé body

SPECIAL FEATURES

A fold-out wood veneer armrest with glass holders adds a touch of class.

RUNNING GEAR

Steering: Worm-and-nut

Front suspension: Wishbones with radius links, torsion bars, telescopic shock absorbers and anti-roll bar

Rear suspension: Rigid axle with semi-elliptic leaf springs and telescopic shock absorbers

Brakes: Discs (front), drums (rear)

Wheels: Steel, 38.1cm (15in) dia

Tyres: 6.70 x 15

DIMENSIONS

Length: 4.74m (186.5in)

Width: 1.78m (70.0in)

Height: 1.46m (57.3in)

Wheelbase: 218cm (110.5in)

Track: 140.5cm (55.3in) (front), 142cm (56.0in) (rear)

Weight: 1578kg (3479lbs)

Rover **SD1 VITESSE**

By tuning the V8, fitting fuel injection, a neat bodykit and uprating the tyres, wheels and suspension, Rover turned the 3.5-litre version of its SD1 luxury hatchback into one of Europe's most enjoyable performance sedans of the early 1980s.

"...easy to drive fast."

"The Vitesse is quite a large car by European standards, but it just seems to shrink around the driver, feeling much smaller and very agile. It's easy to drive fast with a chassis that communicates what all the wheels are doing and what the limits of road holding are. It gives confidence to exploit the performance by turning in sharply, staying flat through the turns and being very predictable when the tail swings out. It rides better the faster it goes and remains perfectly stable."

The wooden steering wheel has been fitted as an option, but adds to the sporty feel.

Milestones

1976 Rover launches the SD1,
a stylish hatchback. Powered by the ex-GM 3.5-liter V8 engine giving 155bhp, it reaches 201km/h (125mph), for a 0–96km/h (0–60mph) time of 8.5-seconds.

The Ferrari Daytona-esque lines of the SD1 had instant appeal.

1981 Rover adds the Vanden Plas
version to the top of the SD1 range. It is soon followed by a 2.4-liter turbo diesel giving 90 bhp.

TWR prepared SD1s were highly competitive in touring car racing during the 1980s.

1983 A substantial increase
in power and uprated brakes and suspension produces the fastest SD1 yet, the fuel-injected Vitesse.

1986 After a decade in production,
Rover releases the twin-plenum Vitesse, an even better performer. However, only 200 of these are built before SD1 production ends.

UNDER THE SKIN

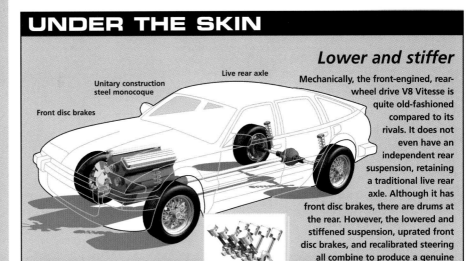

Unitary construction steel monocoque

Live rear axle

Front disc brakes

Fuel-injected V8

Lower and stiffer

Mechanically, the front-engined, rear-wheel drive V8 Vitesse is quite old-fashioned compared to its rivals. It does not even have an independent rear suspension, retaining a traditional live rear axle. Although it has front disc brakes, there are drums at the rear. However, the lowered and stiffened suspension, uprated front disc brakes, and recalibrated steering all combine to produce a genuine high performance car that had enormous appeal.

THE POWER PACK

Injected V8

By the time of the Vitesse, Rover had enormous experience with the all-alloy 3.5-litre V8 engine that it had bought from GM. To begin with, Rover adapted it for twin carburetors, but for the Vitesse more serious modifications were made. Lucas electronic fuel injection was fitted and the intake ports were reprofiled to improve gas flow into the combustion chambers. These changes had a dramatic effect, boosting power to 190bhp and increasing torque to 220lb-ft. In 1986, a Twin Plenum intake was fitted as a homologation exercise, though on paper, power remained unchanged.

Final fling

Named for the French word for speed, the Vitesse was the last hurrah for Rover's slick SD1. Although the final Twin Plenum models got rave reviews, any Vitesse model stands out as a low production special destined to become a collectible commodity.

Vitesse models were only built for three years (a 1983 model is shown).

Rover **SD1 VITESSE**

In the 1970s, Rover wanted a bold, aggressive shape for its new sedans. However, the company waited six years before fitting the tuned V8 engine, which gave it the high performance it really deserved.

V8 engine

The GM-designed 3.5-litre V8 was ideal for Rover's top-of-the-range models in England. It was compact, thanks to its very short stroke (71mm/2.80 inches) and could be easily tuned. Its displacement could be also easily increased to 3.9 and 4.5 litres.

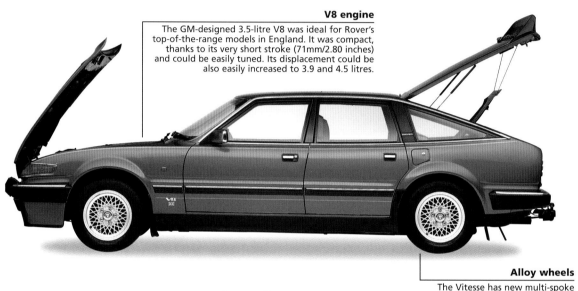

Alloy wheels

The Vitesse has new multi-spoke alloy wheels. At 16.5cm (6.5in) wide and 38cm (15in) in diameter, they are bigger than those on the standard V8 models. They carry low-profile 205/60 VR15 tyres.

Rear spoiler

With its 56:44 percent front/rear weight distribution, the Vitesse required a new large rear wing to provide some more downforce at high speed. In addition, it is also said to help improve the car's aerodynamics from a 0.39Cd to what was then an impressive 0.36Cd.

Lowered ride height

To improve its handling, Rover lowered the
Vitesse by 25mm (1in) and the spring and shock
rates were stiffened by 20 per cent. Variable
rate springs were used to give a compliant ride
at low speeds and assist cornering.

Rear self-levelling

The standard SD1 had a Boge Nivomat self-levelling
rear suspension to keep the car even when fully
loaded. This was retained for the Vitesse, but many
owners changed it in favour of conventional shocks.

1983 Rover SD1 Vitesse

ENGINE

Type: V8

Construction: Alloy block with dry, cast-iron liners and alloy heads

Valve gear: Two valves per cylinder operated by a single V-mounted camshaft with pushrods, rockers, and hydraulic lifters

Bore and stroke: 89mm (3.50in) x 71mm (2.80in)

Displacement: 3528cc (215ci)

Compression ratio: 9.75:1

Induction system: Lucas L electronic fuel injection

Maximum power: 190bhp at 5280rpm

Maximum torque: 220lb-ft at 4000rpm

Top Speed: 217km/h (135mph)

0–96km (0–60mph): 7.1 sec

TRANSMISSION

Five-speed manual

BODY/CHASSIS

Unitary monocoque construction with four-door hatchback body

SPECIAL FEATURES

The rear light cluster has a distinctive ribbed design.

RUNNING GEAR

Steering: Rack-and-pinion

Front suspension: MacPherson struts with lower control arms and anti-roll bar

Rear suspension: Live axle with trailing arms, torque tube, vault linkage, coil springs and telescopic shock absorbers

Brakes: Vented discs, 25.7cm (10.1in) dia. (front), drums, 22.9cm (9.0in) dia. (rear)

Wheels: Alloy, 16.5cm (6.5in) x 38.1cm (15in)

Tyres: Goodyear NCT, 205/60 VR15

DIMENSIONS

Length: 4.73m (186.3in)

Width: 1.77m (69.6in)

Height: 1.38m (54.3in)

Wheelbase: 281cm (110.8in)

Track: 151cm (59.3in) (front and rear)

Weight: 1440kg (3175lbs)

Triumph **SPITFIRE**

In the 1960s, Triumph needed a small sports car to rival the MG Midget. Named after a World War II fighter plane, the Spitfire was a convincing package, with sharp styling by Michelotti and enthusiastic performance.

"...agile in action."

"The Spitfire is agile in action, the four-cylinder engine working hard to produce sporty acceleration and a near-160km/h (100mph) top speed. The crisp transmission invites frequent gear shifts and overdrive makes for relaxed motorway driving. The steering is light and accurate, while the brakes are certainly incisive. The Spitfire's Achilles' heel, however, is its handling. The swing axle rear suspension can lead to wayward oversteer."

The Spitfire's interior is spacious compared with its rivals from MG and Austin-Healey.

Milestones

The GT6 was a coupé version of the Spitfire with a 2.0-liter straight-six engine.

The Mk IV Spitfire was entirely reskinned and was available with a 1500cc (92ci) engine.

UNDER THE SKIN

Swing axle rear suspension

Front disc brakes

Separate chassis

Sedan-sourced engine

Hark the Herald

The Spitfire was based on the separate chassis of the Triumph Herald sedan to keep costs down. The Herald chassis was shortened, and as many parts as possible came from the earlier car, including the engine, steering, transmission and suspension. The swing axle rear suspension is not ideal for sports cars, and Triumph switched to revised leaf-to-pivot rear suspension for the Mk IV. Standard front disc brakes and optional overdrive were available from 1963.

THE POWER PACK

Twin-carb four

The Spitfire's powerplant dates back to the 1953 Standard Eight sedan. The original Spitfire 4 was fitted with a 1147cc (70ci) version of this four-cylinder engine, producing 63bhp. In Mk II form power rose to 67bhp. The Mk III, with its 1296cc (79ci) engine, had an output of 75bhp. Power then began to fall as a result of emission regulations: 63bhp for the Mk IV and just 48–58bhp in the US. Even the larger 1500cc (92ci) engine did not make much impact, registering a mere 52.5–57bhp in US specification.

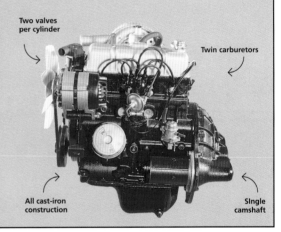

Two valves per cylinder

Twin carburetors

All cast-iron construction

Single camshaft

Best 'Spit'

The model preferred by collectors is the Mk III. Its 75bhp, 1296cc (79ci) engine makes it the fastest of all the Spitfires. It also retains more of the original styling than the later Mk IV, and has raised bumpers that were fitted to satisfy US safety regulations.

The Mk III combines the sharpest styling and peppiest performance.

Triumph **SPITFIRE**

Compared to the cramped MG Midget, the Triumph Spitfire heralded a new beginning for sports car drivers. Nimble and agile, yet willing and exciting to drive, it became one of the best-selling sports cars of all time.

Swing-forward front end

All Spitfires feature a one-piece front end, encompassing the bonnet and front fenders. It swings forward for easy access to the engine and front suspension.

Improved soft-top

The Spitfire was conceived as a traditional-style British sports car with an open roof. The first Spitfires had a completely removable top. However, a much more practical soft-top arrived in 1967 on the Mk III. A detachable steel hardtop was optional.

Rack-and-pinion steering

The very light and direct steering derived from the Herald was remarkable for the tightness of its turning circle. At 7m (23ft), it was the tightest of any production car.

Overdrive option

No other small sports car offered optional overdrive. This Laycock device, operating on third and fourth gears, made highway cruising much more relaxed.

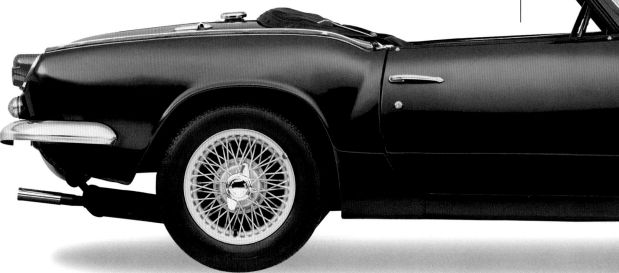

Michelotti styling

One of the main advantages of the Spitfire over the slab-sided MG Midget was its Italian styling by Michelotti. Michelotti was used again in 1970 to restyle the front and rear ends, notably adding a cut-off 'Kamm' tail.

Backbone chassis

The separate chassis is essentially that of a Herald but with the wheelbase shortened by 20.3cm (8in). It is a double-backbone channel-section, with outriggers to support the bodywork on each side.

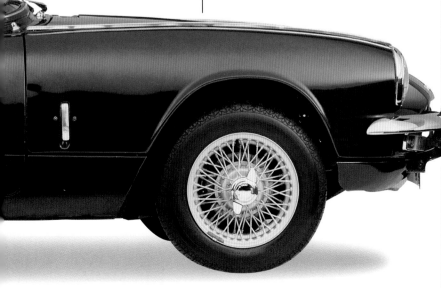

Specifications

1967 Triumph Spitfire Mk III

ENGINE
Type: In-line four-cylinder
Construction: Cast-iron block and head
Valve gear: Two valves per cylinder operated by a single camshaft via pushrods and rockers
Bore and stroke: 74mm (2.90in) x 76mm (2.99in)
Displacement: 1296cc (79ci)
Compression ratio: 8.0:1
Induction system: Twin carburetors
Maximum power: 75bhp at 6000rpm
Maximum torque: 75lb-ft at 4000rpm
Top Speed: 156km/h (97mph)
0–96km (0–60mph): 13.6 sec

TRANSMISSION
Four-speed manual with optional overdrive

BODY/CHASSIS
Separate chassis with two-door open steel body

SPECIAL FEATURES

The bumper was raised on Mk III models to comply with US safety legislation.

RUNNING GEAR
Steering: Rack-and-pinion
Front suspension: Wishbones with coil springs, shock absorbers and anti-roll bar
Rear suspension: Swing axles with transverse leaf springs and shock absorbers
Brakes: Discs (front), drums (rear)
Wheels: Spoked wires, 11.4cm (4.5in) x 33cm (13in)
Tyres: 155/70 SR13

DIMENSIONS
Length: 3.78m (149.0in)
Width: 1.49m (58.6in)
Height: 1.13m (44.3in)
Wheelbase: 211cm (83.0in)
Track: 124cm (49.0 in) (front), 127cm (50.0 in) (rear)
Weight: 762kg (1680lbs)

Triumph **TR6**

To the enthusiast, the TR6 was the final Triumph TR. It was the last to have a separate chassis and more power than grip; a car that needed a real driver to get all the performance out of its old-fashioned design.

"...performance is excellent."

"It helps if you know what you're doing with a TR6. Some cars look after you, but not the TR6. It's easy to get the front-heavy Triumph into corners too fast, but it is well mannered enough for the tail not to come around. The steering is heavy and low geared, and the wheel is at the driver's chest. The ride is harsh and firm and yet the TR6 rises above all that. Straight-line power is excellent, and once you realize the chassis' limitations, it really is great fun."

Simple wooden dashboard is typically British. The steering wheel is right in your lap and gauges clear and easy to read.

Milestones

1953 Triumph TR line starts with the four-cylinder TR2 and progresses through TR3 in 1955, TR3A in 1958, TR4 in 1961 and TR4A in 1961, by which time engine size has grown to 2.2 litres and independent rear suspension has appeared.

TR2 started the famous TR line.

1967 Fitting the 2.5-litre straight-six to the TR produces the TR5. It has Italian styling, like the TR4 and 4A.

1969 Karmann of Germany restyles the front and rear to give the TR6 its characteristic chopped tail and full-width front grille. It has wider wheels than the TR5 and a front anti-roll bar. American spec cars uses two Stromberg carburetors rather than fuel injection for emissions reasons.

1973 The engine characteristics are changed, and power reduced with a different camshaft.

1976 Production ends.

The TR5 uses a straight-six engine.

UNDER THE SKIN

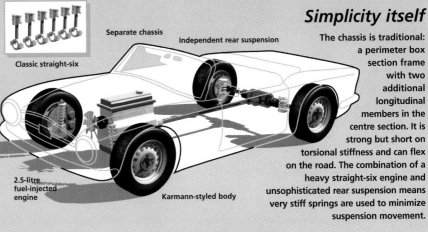

Classic straight-six

Separate chassis

Independent rear suspension

2.5-litre fuel-injected engine

Karmann-styled body

Simplicity itself

The chassis is traditional: a perimeter box section frame with two additional longitudinal members in the centre section. It is strong but short on torsional stiffness and can flex on the road. The combination of a heavy straight-six engine and unsophisticated rear suspension means very stiff springs are used to minimize suspension movement.

THE POWER PACK

Fuel injection

There is little that's advanced about the all-iron straight-six, developed from the Triumph Vitesse 1600 engine of the early 1960s. It is an old-fashioned pushrod engine with one block-mounted camshaft and two overhead valves per cylinder. Even the dimensions are old-fashioned, hence it has a long stroke. It is strong, torquey and smooth – perfectly suited to the TR6. Lucas mechanical fuel injection pushes power to a respectable 150bhp.

Two valves per cylinder

Valves operated by pushrods

Mechanical fuel injection

Iron block and cylinder head

Euro-Brit

Most TR6s were sold in the US, where emission laws ruined engine output, dropping it to 106bhp with twin carburetors. That means the pre-1974 European spec 150bhp car is the one to go for, despite the sometimes troublesome mechanical fuel injection.

Pre-1974 TR6s have a 150bhp fuel-injected engine and the best performance.

Triumph **TR6**

Rugged and uncompromising, crude and old-fashioned, the TR6 was one of the last of its breed and it had enough performance, style and character to make up for all its shortcomings.

Rack-and-pinion steering
British manufacturers were the first to be convinced of the advantages of rack-and-pinion steering, and the TR6 is so equipped.

Straight-six engine
The TR5 and TR6 were the only TRs to have a six-cylinder engine. The earlier cars had four-cylinders, as did the TR7. TR8s had V8s.

Foldaway top
The top is easy to put up and down. When stowed, it fits neatly away behind the seats and fits flush with the bodywork, so it won't spoil the lines of the car.

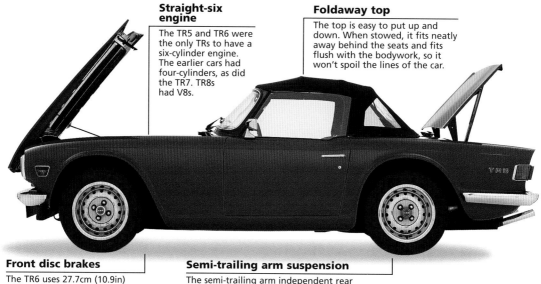

Front disc brakes
The TR6 uses 27.7cm (10.9in) Girling disc brakes in the front, while the rear brakes still use drums.

Semi-trailing arm suspension
The semi-trailing arm independent rear suspension was better than the old TR's live axle but it was not perfect, so Triumph gave it wide (for the time) rear tyres along with stiff springs to limit its movement.

Karmann styling
Karmann skillfully transformed the look of the TR with minimal changes. It added wraparound and squared tail lghts and redesigned the front end.

Overdrive transmission
Although the TR6 has a four-speed transmission, it's equipped with overdrive, operating on the top three ratios to effectively give seven gears.

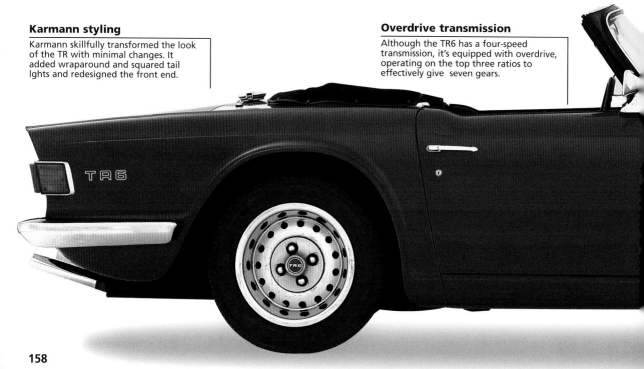

Wishbone front suspension

In Britain, a sports car's front suspension was traditionally double wishbone. The TR6 is no exception.

Dual exhaust

With a straight-six engine, there was no need for twin exhaust tail pipes, but this arrangement improves the rear styling.

Specifications
1969
Triumph TR6

ENGINE
Type: Straight-six
Construction: Cast-iron block and head
Valve gear: Two valves per cylinder operated by single block-mounted camshaft, pushrods and rockers
Bore and stroke: 75mm (2.95in) x 95mm (3.74in)
Displacement: 2498cc (152ci)
Compression ratio: 9.5:1
Induction system: Lucas mechanical fuel injection
Maximum power: 150bhp at 5500 rpm
Maximum torque: 164lb-ft at 3500 rpm
Top Speed: 175km/h (109mph)
0–96km/h (0–60mph): 10.5 sec

TRANSMISSION
Four-speed manual transmission with overdrive on top three ratios

BODY/CHASSIS
Box section perimeter chassis with steel two-door convertible body

SPECIAL FEATURES

Karmann's restyle of the front and rear gave the TR6 a muscular look.

RUNNING GEAR
Steering: Rack-and-pinion
Front suspension: Double wishbones with coil springs, telescopic shocks and anti-roll bar
Rear suspension: Semi-trailing arms with coil springs and telescopic shocks
Brakes: Discs 27.7cm (10.9in) dia. (front), drums (rear)
Wheels: Steel disc, 14cm (5.5in) x 38.1cm (15in)

DIMENSIONS
Length: 4.04m (159in)
Width: 1.47m (58in)
Height: 1.27m (50in)
Wheelbase: 224cm (88in)
Track: 125cm (49.3in) (front), 124cm (48.8in) (rear)
Weight: 1122kg (2473lbs)

Triumph **STAG**

Launched in 1970, the Stag was intended to move Triumph into the sporty grand touring segment. Gutsy, handsome, fast and practical, it became an automotive icon through the 1970s.

"...refined and comfortable."

"Because it was an entirely unique car in 1970, it was difficult at the time to appreciate the Stag's attributes. The V8 engine is smooth, with a refined rumble resonating from the exhaust. Acceleration is average at best. The Stag is more at home high-speed cruising than standing-start drag racing. The coil-sprung suspension results in a comfortable ride and, although it rolls through turns, the car is easy to control."

As befitting a grand tourer, the Stag has leather upholstery and a wood dash.

Milestones

1970 Triumph boldly launches its
Michelotti-styled V8-powered Stag. It is the first Triumph sports car to embody unitary construction and the first to be powered by a V8 engine.

1971 Triumph begins to export the
Stag to the US.

Also styled by Michelotti, the gutsy TR6 was far removed from the refined Stag.

1973 A Mark II version is finally introduced. It has a
more refined V8 engine, better steering, improved seating and a different soft top.

Dolomite Sprints use a slant four, which is essentially half of the Stag's 3.0-litre V8.

1977 The final Stags are produced
after a relatively small production run.

UNDER THE SKIN

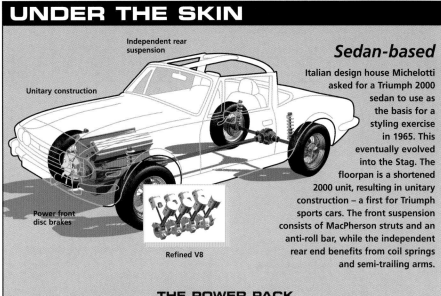

Independent rear suspension

Unitary construction

Power front disc brakes

Refined V8

Sedan-based

Italian design house Michelotti asked for a Triumph 2000 sedan to use as the basis for a styling exercise in 1965. This eventually evolved into the Stag. The floorpan is a shortened 2000 unit, resulting in unitary construction – a first for Triumph sports cars. The front suspension consists of MacPherson struts and an anti-roll bar, while the independent rear end benefits from coil springs and semi-trailing arms.

THE POWER PACK

Home-grown

Triumph remained fiercely independent even after its merger with Leyland. Thus, when it came to fitting an engine into the Stag, Triumph decided to use its own V8, a single overhead-cam, 3.0-litre unit with alloy cylinder heads. In 1973, the unit received reshaped combustion chambers and higher compression pistons with domed tops, making it both smoother and quieter. However, early engines suffered from cooling and reliability problems, which severely tarnished the Stag's image.

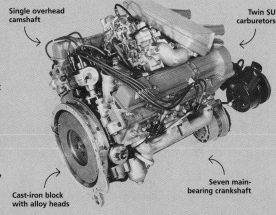

Single overhead camshaft

Twin SU carburetors

Cast-iron block with alloy heads

Seven main-bearing crankshaft

Mk II Stag

Post-1973 Stags, with a reworked V8 engine, improved seating and attractive five-spoke wheels, are preferred by collectors. The best investment is an all-original, low-mileage Mk II. If well maintained, Stags can be very reliable.

The best buy is the later, post-1973 Stag Mk II.

Triumph **STAG**

The Stag may have gained a reputation as being a fragile sports car – and an unreliable one at that – but its mix of good road manners, Italian styling, rarity and practicality make it an attractive classic today.

V8 power

Despite its refinement, the 145bhp V8 was the Stag's Achilles' heel. The high mounted water pump often results in the engine overheating, a notorious Stag fault. Furthermore, the engine has a tendency to blow cylinder head gaskets and poor-quality control led to many warranty claims on blown engines.

BMW-like suspension

The Stag's suspension – MacPherson struts and lower wishbones up front and semi-trailing arms at the rear – is strongly reminiscent of contemporary BMW's.

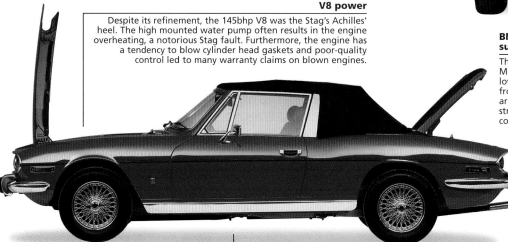

Italian styling

The attractive final shape was a combination of Michelotti and Triumph ideas. Prototypes were shuttled between the Triumph factory and the Italian design house in Turin for modifications. The padded roll-over bar was a unique feature, as were the generously-sized rear seats.

Choice of tops

Customers could specify whether they wanted soft or hard tops (or both). The soft top worked very effectively with the T-bar, and the hard top. While it looked very attractive, the top was often criticized for being heavy and cumbersome to fit.

Four-seater layout

The notion of a full four-seater convertible was very unusual in Europe. The Stag embodied a belief at the time that Leyland should be setting trends, not following them. It was thought that the Stag was the type of car that would sell well in the US, but this did not prove to be the case.

Unitary construction

Because the Stag used a much-modified version of the 2000 Sedan floorpan, it became the first Triumph sports car to use integral unitary construction. This improved handling and reduced chassis flex.

Specifications

1977 Triumph Stag

ENGINE
Type: V8
Construction: Cast-iron block and aluminium heads
Valve gear: Two valves per cylinder operated by a single overhead camshaft
Bore and stroke: 86mm (3.38in) x 65mm (2.54in)
Displacement: 2997cc (183ci)
Compression ratio: 8.8:1
Induction system: Two Stromberg carburetors
Maximum power: 145bhp at 5500 rpm
Maximum torque: 170lb-ft at 3500 rpm
Top Speed: 190km/h (118mph)
0–96km/h (0–60mph): 9.3 sec

TRANSMISSION
Four-speed manual plus overdrive or three-speed automatic

BODY/CHASSIS
Integral chassis with two-door steel convertible body

SPECIAL FEATURES

The four-speed overdrive transmission came from the 2000 sedan.

RUNNING GEAR
Steering: Rack-and-pinion
Front suspension: MacPherson struts with lower wishbones, coil springs, shock absorbers and anti-roll bar
Rear suspension: Semi-trailing arms with coil springs and shock absorbers
Brakes: Discs (front), drums (rear)
Wheels: Steel wire, 35.6cm (14in) dia.
Tyres: 185 x 14

DIMENSIONS
Length: 4.42m (174.0in)
Width: 1.61m (63.5in)
Height: 1.26m (49.5in)
Wheelbase: 254cm (100in)
Track: 133cm (52.6in) (front), 135cm (53.0in) (rear)
Weight: 1268kg (2795lbs)

Triumph **TR7**

Last of a long and distinguished line of TR Triumph sports cars, the TR7 was somewhat maligned because of its radical styling and poor quality control. Nevertheless, it was a runaway sales success because it was such a joy to drive.

"...fun, with a willing engine."

"It's no wonder that drivers of earlier TRs don't like the TR7; it's a completely different car than what they're used to. The 1970s-styled cabin is wider but is still a sports car's – able to be easily thrown around. It is fun, with a willing engine. The ride is firm but not uncomfortable, and the steering is communicative, if a little low-geared for spirited wheel-twirling. Its weak link, however, is the brakes – four-wheel discs would have easily fixed this."

The black plastic interior is very 1970s, but the TR7 is more user-friendly than earlier models.

Milestones

1975 The world is shocked by the replacement of the traditional TR6 with the radical TR7, offered in coupé form only for the US market.

1976 Sales begin in other markets and a five-speed transmission becomes optional.

Triumph's TR6 was the last of the traditional TR sports cars.

1977 As British Leyland's official rally car, the TR7 scores a win in the Boucles de Spa event in Belgium.

1979 Five speeds are standardized and a new convertible model is launched.

Developed from the TR7, the TR8 uses a 3.5-litre V8 engine.

1980 The V8-powered TR8 arrives.

1981 Triumph's Liverpool factory closes and the TR7 is officially retired.

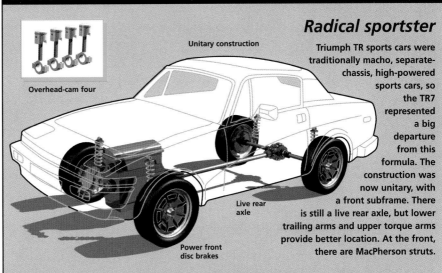

Overhead-cam four

Unitary construction

Live rear axle

Power front disc brakes

Radical sportster

Triumph TR sports cars were traditionally macho, separate-chassis, high-powered sports cars, so the TR7 represented a big departure from this formula. The construction was now unitary, with a front subframe. There is still a live rear axle, but lower trailing arms and upper torque arms provide better location. At the front, there are MacPherson struts.

THE POWER PACK

Cammer controversy

Purists may have criticized the demise of the TR6's gutsy six-cylinder engine, but the TR7's controversial four-cylinder unit was hardly a bad replacement. It was an overhead-cam, alloy-headed engine that had seen plenty of service in the Triumph Dolomite sedan. In the TR7, however, it did without the 16-valve head of the Dolomite Sprint. In Europe, the 2.0-litre, twin-carburetor engine produced 105bhp, but in the US, output was down to 90bhp due to strict emissions requirements. US buyers would have to wait until the Rover V8-powered TR8 was launched, for the TR7 to get the performance it truly deserved.

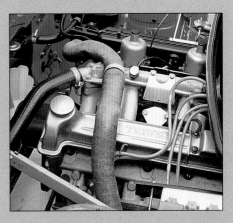

Drophead

If you ignore the raunchy V8-powered TR8, you have a straight choice between the TR7 fixed-head coupe and the convertible. The latter is the obvious winner of this contest, with its better looks, open-air fun and greater collector status.

A convertible was finally sold along with the coupé in 1979.

Triumph **TR7**

Nothing looked anything like the TR7 when it arrived in 1975. Diehard Triumph fans had difficulty accepting it, but the new TR sold extremely well in the US, which was its main market.

Impact bumpers

The TR7 was designed during the height of the US Federal car safety programme. As such, it came with full-size rubberized safety bumpers, which it never lost in its six-year production run.

Four- to five-speed transmission

Early cars were fitted with tough four-speed manual transmissions from the Morris Marina. Triumph soon adopted the five-speed unit from the Rover 3500, initially as an option but later as standard equipment.

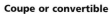

Coupe or convertible

Triumph's original plan had been to make a drop-top TR7 from the start, but concerns about a possible ban on open cars in the US led Triumph to launch the new sports car as a fixed-head only in 1975. The convertible did not arrive until 1979.

Live rear axle

Triumph opted to use a simple live rear axle in the TR7. It is located by lower trailing arms and upper oblique radius arms and suspended by coil springs.

Controversial styling

Triumph described its new coupé as 'the shape of things to come' and as 'the bold wedge line of the great international sports racers.' The bold wedge shape was penned by Harris Mann.

Specifications

1975 Triumph TR7

ENGINE

Type: In-line four-cylinder

Construction: Cast-iron cylinder block and aluminium cylinder head

Valve gear: Two valves per cylinder operated by single overhead camshaft

Bore and stroke: 90mm (3.55in) x 78mm (3.07in)

Displacement: 1998cc (122ci)

Compression ratio: 8.0:1

Induction system: Two Stromberg carburetors

Maximum power: 90bhp at 5000rpm

Maximum torque: 106lb-ft at 3000rpm

Top Speed: 177km/h (110mph)

0–96km (0–60mph): 11.2 sec

TRANSMISSION

Four-speed manual or three-speed automatic (five-speed optional from 1976, standard from 1979)

BODY/CHASSIS

Unitary monocoque construction with steel two-door coupé body

SPECIAL FEATURES

Export versions, particularly US cars, had different-pattern wheels.

Aerodynamics and US lighting laws dictated pop-up headlights on the TR7.

RUNNING GEAR

Steering: Rack-and-pinion

Front suspension: MacPherson struts with lower lateral links, coil springs, shock absorbers and anti-roll bar

Rear suspension: Live axle with trailing arms, radius arms, coil springs, shock absorbers and anti-roll bar

Brakes: Discs (front), drums (rear)

Wheels: Steel 33cm (13in) dia.

Tyres: 175/70 HR13

DIMENSIONS

Length: 4.17m (164.5in)

Width: 1.68m (66.2in)

Height: 1.27m (49.9in)

Wheelbase: 216cm (85.0in)

Track: 141cm (55.5in) (front), 140cm (55.3in) (rear)

Weight: 1016kg (2240lbs)

TVR **GRIFFITH**

The Griffith is a world away from TVR's kit-car origins. The quality is high, the design outstanding and the performance from its latest 5-litre V8 engine nothing short of staggering.

"...guarantees excitement."

"More than 300bhp in a light car that has a short wheelbase guarantees excitement and the Griffith delivers a huge amount of it. Lurid power is only a touch of the throttle away, as the power overcomes the grip of the big rear tyres despite the limited slip differential. Before the power-assisted steering became available, it took an acute combination of strength and finesse to control such behaviour. You also need a firm hand for the gear shifter and a strong leg for the clutch, but the Griffith's breathtaking acceleration makes it all worth the effort."

Smart and stylish dashboard of the Griffith uses many recognizable switches and gauges.

Milestones

1963 The distant ancestor of the current Griffith has a Ford V8 and is named after US Ford dealer Jack Griffith. It can reach 257km/h (160mph), but the car is very difficult to drive fast.

By the late 1980s, the wedge-shaped TVRs were beginning to look dated.

1990 TVR builds another Griffith, as a show car for the British Motor Show. Reaction is enthusiastic, so TVR decides to put the Griffith into production.

The Racing Tuscan showed TVR's potential.

1992 The production Griffith debuts. It is designed to use a variety of Rover V8 engines, from a 'basic' 240bhp version, through a 250bhp stage and up to the 280bhp 4.3-litre version.

1993 An even more powerful Griffith appears. The engine is enlarged to litres, to form the 340-bhp Griffith 500.

UNDER THE SKIN

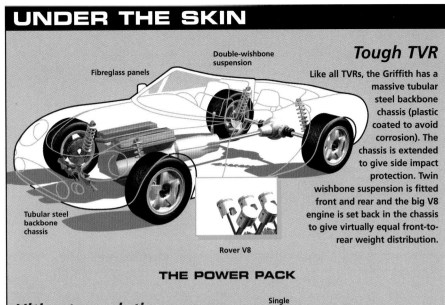

Fibreglass panels

Double-wishbone suspension

Tubular steel backbone chassis

Rover V8

Tough TVR

Like all TVRs, the Griffith has a massive tubular steel backbone chassis (plastic coated to avoid corrosion). The chassis is extended to give side impact protection. Twin wishbone suspension is fitted front and rear and the big V8 engine is set back in the chassis to give virtually equal front-to-rear weight distribution.

THE POWER PACK

Ultimate evolution

The 5-litre V8 in the Griffith 500 is the ultimate evolution of the Rover V8 still used in Range Rovers. The original design was from General Motors in the US, but TVR has taken the all-alloy pushrod V8 out to 4997cc (305ci), reinforced the block and extracted well over twice the power of the first 3.5-litre engines from the 1960s. The Rover V8, in various forms, has been the mainstay of TVR since the 1980s and is still used alongside TVR's new AJP V8.

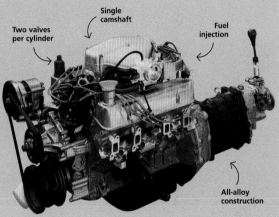

Two valves per cylinder

Single camshaft

Fuel injection

All-alloy construction

Best of British

The Griffith's stunning looks don't come from an expensive Italian styling house or from computer-aided design, but from the eye of TVR boss Peter Wheeler and engineer John Ravenscroft. They sculpted a full-size foam model until they arrived at the Griffith's stunning shape.

Designed in-house, the Griffith looks spectacular from any angle.

TVR GRIFFITH 🇬🇧

The Griffith is just like a modern-day AC Cobra, the concept being a very large powerful engine in a small convertible. Like the Cobra, there's very little to rival the Griffith.

Fibreglass bodywork
The fibreglass body is bolted to the tubular steel chassis to make a stronger, stiffer overall structure.

Flat-mounted radiator
The radiator is mounted at a very shallow angle and the air is drawn through it by twin electric fans. There was room to allow this because the engine is set so far back.

Rover transmission
Sensibly, the TVR use the same tough, five-speed transmission that Rover used in the fastest of its V8-engined cars, the Vitesse.

Tubular steel chassis
The tubular steel chassis is designed to give the Griffith an extremely strong central backbone, which is the way TVR has always designed its chassis.

Larger rear wheels
To cope with its huge power output, the Griffith has larger, 19cm (7.5in) x 40.6cm (16in) OZ Racing split-rim alloy rear wheels.

Optional leather trim
If you want your Griffith to be luxurious as well as very fast, leather seats and trim are an option.

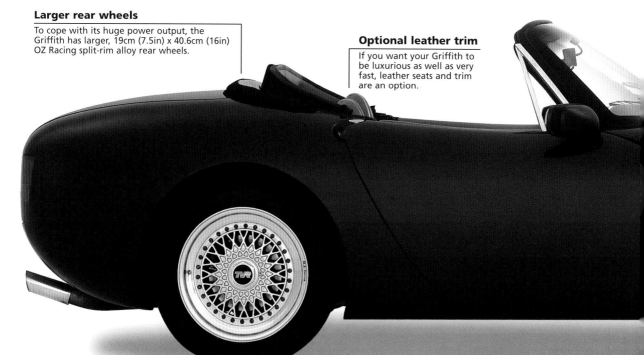

Equal weight distribution

With the engine set well back in the chassis, the heavy Rover transmission is near the centre of the car: The weight distribution is almost ideal at 51 per cent front, 49 per cent rear.

Wishbone suspension

Twin wishbone suspension is used all around on the Griffith. The rear suspension is very similar to that found on the mighty TVR Tuscan racers.

Ford Sierra final drive

The final drive housing is actually a Ford Sierra part, but the gears inside are much stronger, with a Quaife limited slip differential to reduce wheelspin and help traction.

Specifications
1993 TVR Griffith 500

ENGINE
Type: V8, overhead valve
Construction: Alloy block and heads
Valve gear: Two valves per cylinder operated by single block-mounted camshaft via pushrods and rockers
Bore and stroke: 90mm (3.54in) x 90mm (3.54in)
Displacement: 4997cc (305ci)
Compression ratio: 10:1
Induction system: Electronic fuel injection
Maximum power: 340bhp at 5500rpm
Maximum torque: 351lb-ft at 4000rpm
Top Speed: 269km/h (167mph)
0–96km/h (0–60mph): 4.4 sec

TRANSMISSION
Five-speed manual

BODY/CHASSIS
Fibreglass two-door, two-seat convertible with tubular steel backbone chassis

SPECIAL FEATURES

The V8 has massive exhaust headers which have to be routed around the front of the engine.

Small door handles are neatly recessed so the lines of the car are not spoiled.

RUNNING GEAR
Steering: Rack-and-pinion
Front suspension: Twin wishbones, coil springs, telescopic shocks and anti-roll bar
Rear suspension: Twin wishbones, coil springs and telescopic shocks
Brakes: Disc, vented 25.9cm (10.2in) dia. (front), solid 27.2cm (10.7in) dia. (rear)
Wheels: Alloy OZ, 17.8cm (7in) x 38.1cm (15in) (front), 19cm (7.5in) x 40.6cm (16in) (rear)
Tyres: 215/50ZR15 (front), 225/50ZR16 (rear)

DIMENSIONS
Length: 3.96m (156.1in)
Width: 1.94m (76.5in)
Height: 1.19m (46.7in)
Wheelbase: 148.3cm (58.4in)
Track: 147cm (58in) (front), 148cm (58.4in) (rear)
Weight: 1045kg (2304lbs)

TVR **CHIMAERA**

Although milder than the fearsome Griffith, the Chimaera is still a seriously fast sports car, built using the same recipe that makes early Corvettes great: a separate chassis, fibreglass body and a big V8 driving the rear wheels.

"...made for skilful drivers."

"Chimaeras are made for skilful drivers. There's a lot of power for a car with such a short wheelbase (35.6cm/14in shorter than a Corvette), and it's set up to give instant response to the incredibly quick steering. It's easily steered on the throttle, too. The V8 sounds great, and is accompanied by flexible power that gives serious overtaking ability. What's more, the ride is nowhere near as hard as you'd expect and the TVR feels immensely solid."

Classy gauges and a chunky wheel hint at the Chimaera's potent performance.

Milestones

1993 TVR launches the Chimaera, which
fills a hole in its range between the popular 'S' convertible and the mighty 5.0-litre Griffith.

The Griffith was the first of the modern wave of TVRs.

1995 At the top of the Chimaera range
now is the 5.0-litre version with the bored and stroked Rover engine from the Griffith 500, giving 340bhp.

The Cerbera currently tops the TVR range.

1997 TVR fills a gap
between the 240bhp 4.0-litre and 340bhp 5.0-litre with the 4.5-litre version. The new engine is a long-stroke version of the 4.0-litre and gives 285bhp at 5500 rpm and 310lb-ft of torque at 4250 rpm. It has the same improvements as the 5.0-litre car, so there are bigger brakes, and new wheels that carry the Bridgestone S-02 tyres are now fitted to all TVRs.

UNDER THE SKIN

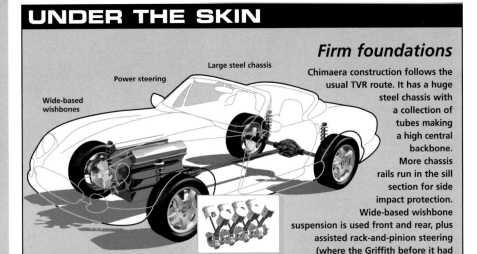

Large steel chassis

Power steering

Wide-based wishbones

All-alloy V8

Firm foundations

Chimaera construction follows the usual TVR route. It has a huge steel chassis with a collection of tubes making a high central backbone. More chassis rails run in the sill section for side impact protection. Wide-based wishbone suspension is used front and rear, plus assisted rack-and-pinion steering (where the Griffith before it had none) and four-wheel disc brakes.

THE POWER PACK

GM development

Although TVR now has its own V8 engine design, the V8s used in the Chimaera are developments of the old all-alloy ex-Buick V8 sold to Rover. The engine is a simple design with a single V-mounted camshaft, push-rods, rockers and hydraulic lifters to actuate two valves per cylinder. Rover stretched it from 3.5 litres to 4.0 litres by increasing the bore in the alloy block, but in the TVR installation the compression ratio is increased to a high 9.8:1 and power to 240bhp.

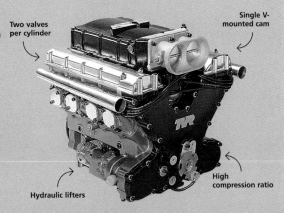

Two valves per cylinder

Single V-mounted cam

High compression ratio

Hydraulic lifters

Top choice

The ultimate Chimaera is the 5.0-litre, which has the biggest stretch of the old Rover engine. It takes power up to 340bhp and torque to 320lb-ft. Naturally, performance rockets too, with a top speed of 265km/h (165mph) and a 0–96km/h (0–60mph) time of 4.1 seconds.

The 5.0-litre Chimaera is an exclusive beast that should be handled with care.

TVR CHIMAERA

Stunning looks as well as performance set the Chimaera apart. TVR styling is all carried out in-house in Blackpool, with traditional clay full-size models sculpted until the effect is just right.

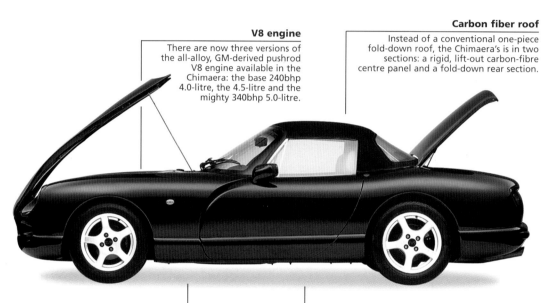

V8 engine

There are now three versions of the all-alloy, GM-derived pushrod V8 engine available in the Chimaera: the base 240bhp 4.0-litre, the 4.5-litre and the mighty 340bhp 5.0-litre.

Carbon fiber roof

Instead of a conventional one-piece fold-down roof, the Chimaera's is in two sections: a rigid, lift-out carbon-fibre centre panel and a fold-down rear section.

Five-speed transmission

In place of the transmission from the Rover SD-1 sedan, TVR chose a Borg-Warner five-speed unit. Its overdrive-fifth gives a relaxed 44km/h (27.5mph) per 1000 revs in top.

Separate chassis

All TVRs have a separate chassis. It is an immensely strong construction of tubular steel that is so rigid there is virtually no cowl shake.

Rack-and-pinion steering

Rack-and-pinion steering is almost universal in sports cars, but what sets the TVR's apart is the extreme quickness of the rack. It is very high-geared, with only 1.9 turns lock to lock, making the car highly controllable in a slide.

Equal weight distribution

Mounting the engine well back in the chassis results in 50/50 weight distribution front and rear. This, plus short front and rear overhangs, give the Chimaera excellent handling.

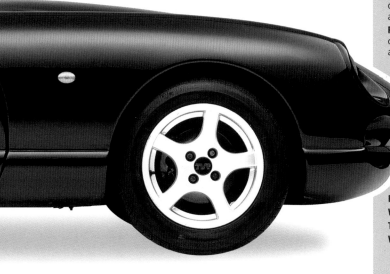

Specifications

1998 TVR Chimaera

ENGINE

Type: V8

Construction: Alloy block and heads

Valve gear: Two valves per cylinder operated by a single camshaft with pushrods and rocker arms

Bore and stroke: 94mm (3.70in) x 71mm (2.80in)

Displacement: 3950cc (241ci)

Compression ratio: 9.8:1

Induction system: Electronic fuel injection

Maximum power: 240bhp at 5250 rpm

Maximum torque: 270lb-ft at 4000 rpm

Top Speed: 254km/h (158mph)

0–96km (0–60mph): 5.2 sec

TRANSMISSION

Five-speed manual

BODY/CHASSIS

Separate tubular-steel backbone chassis with fibreglass two-seater convertible body

SPECIAL FEATURES

The rear of the roof folds into the boot, where the centre section can be stored.

All TVRs are styled in-house at the company's Blackpool base.

RUNNING GEAR

Steering: Rack-and-pinion

Front suspension: Double wishbones with coil springs, telescopic shock absorbers and anti-roll bar

Rear suspension: Double wishbones with coil springs, telescopic shock absorbers and anti-roll bar

Brakes: Vented discs, 26cm (10.2in) dia. (front), 27.2cm (10.7in) dia. (rear)

Wheels: Cast-alloy, 17.8cm (7in) x 38.1cm (15in) (front), 17.8cm (7in) x 40.6cm (16in) (rear)

Tyres: Bridgestone S-02, 205/60 ZR15 (front), 225/55 ZR16 (rear)

DIMENSIONS

Length: 4.55m (179.1in)

Width: 1.94m (76.2in)

Height: 1.28m (50.2in)

Wheelbase: 250cm (98.4in)

Track: 146cm (57.5in) (front and rear)

Weight: 1025kg (2260lbs)

Index